Good, Good Father is
Fatherhood of God, t
speaking terms with I   ..., as all Christians
should be. If asked, what is particularly new about the
'New Covenant,' I always reply, the revelation of God as
our Heavenly Father. Oh, to be sure, this truth is found in
the Old Testament, but only faintly. When Jesus taught His
disciples to pray, saying, 'Our Father in heaven' (Matt. 5:8),
I think there must have been a small reverberation as jaws
dropped! How exquisite that we are adopted children—'sons
of God'! Yes, the masculine because in New Testament times
daughters did not inherit and the whole point of being a
son is that sons are heirs of God, jointly so with Jesus (Rom.
8:17). Dr. Chase writes with a flare that makes this book a
page-turner. But more than that, he makes us glad that the
Sovereign God of the Universe is our Father. And for that, I
am grateful to him. More than I can say.

Derek W. H. Thomas

Senior Minister, First Presbyterian Church, Columbia,
South Carolina
Chancellor's Professor, Reformed Theological Seminary
Teaching Fellow, Ligonier Ministries

For some Reformed evangelicals, confronting the world
with the harder parts of biblical truth has become a higher
theological priority than basking in the noonday warmth of
the goodness of God the Father. Here is an invitation to take
comfort, relax and enjoy the truth that God's love for you
and me has no limit and finds its ultimate manifestation in
the death and resurrection of Jesus Christ.

Jonny Dyer

All Souls, Langham Place, London

Very few are the number of Christian authors who write with the care of a pastor, the skill of a teacher, the wisdom of a mentor, and the precision of an orthodox theologian. The Rev. Dr. Charley Chase is one of those select few. In *Good, Good Father*, Dr. Chase sits down beside you and looks into your eyes; and out of an encyclopaedic grasp of the Bible, with the passion of a dear friend, the calm assurance of an old sage, and the humor of innumerable anecdotes—spun from the porch chair, Charley assures you that God is good every day, all day.

Michael L. Carreker
Rector of the Parish Church of All Souls
Teacher of Humanities, St. David's School, Raleigh, North Carolina

I count it an honor and privilege to recommend *Good, Good Father*, to you. Charley Chase is a friend who walks closer than a brother. He has been that brother to me in the midst of some of my family's darkest days. What an encourager he is! He identifies with people on the mountaintops and in the valleys of life. Charley has the ability to point us to God's promises, helping us to keep sight of the love of our Creator...no matter what! I pray you will get this book, read it, and discover God's faithfulness in all ways. He truly is a good, good, Father!

Bob Hoffman
Head Men's Basketball Coach, University of Central Oklahoma,
Edmond, Oklahoma

Good, Good Father explores a grand theme: abiding in God's fatherly care through Jesus our Lord. In twenty-six short meditations, readers are invited to experience the joy of knowing the God who lavishes His love on His adopted children. Identifying the promises of our heavenly Father and learning to claim them is the privilege Charley Chase wants every reader to enjoy. His scripture expositions are clear, his illustrations sparkle, and his plentiful quotations draw on the treasures of Reformed writers who have thought deeply about God's fatherly love and care for His dear children.

Charles M. Wingard
Associate Professor of Pastoral Theology and Dean of Students, Reformed Theological Seminary, Jackson, Mississippi

C.L. Chase's *Good, Good Father* is an important, practical, accessible exploration of the New Testament's theme of the Fatherhood of God. C.L. Chase makes the case that realizing that God is our Father is the key to unlocking greater blessing as a Christian. Read and enjoy!

Josh Moody
Senior pastor, College Church, Wheaton, Illinois
President and founder of God Centered Life Ministries

Through this book, C.L Chase has provided me with the missing puzzle piece I've needed for living the 'abundant life' Christ died to give us. Like a good Presbyterian, I have delighted in the truth that: 'God is a Spirit, infinite, eternal, and unchangeable...' (WSC). Yet, as beautiful as these truths are, there has been a disconnect in experiencing God as my Father. As my friend Charley points out, 'Jesus' habitat was God as His Abba, Father.' Read this book to discover how to make that your habitat as well!

Cheryl Lutz
Founder at Securely Held Ministries, Atlanta, Georgia

Believers often greet one another with a simple but profound statement: God is good. The expected answer to that greeting is also profound: 'All the time.' To insure our confidence in the integrity of these statements that 'God is good all the time' I commend to you the systematic study of God's goodness encountered in this volume. Enjoy this thoughtful presentation from God's Word that allows us to live confidently by the grace of God as revealed from the Word of God in *Good, Good Father*.

Harry L. Reeder III

Teaching Pastor, Briarwood Presbyterian Church, Birmingham, Alabama

My dear friend Charley Chase has masterfully described God's love for His children in *Good, Good Father*. Offering unique insights gleaned from a lifetime of walking with the Lord, experiencing life's heartaches and joys, Charley lovingly reassures the believer that the One to whom we entrust our lives is indeed greatly to be praised. Of all his many talents, Charley's greatest gift is the ability to uplift a fellow traveler with a well-timed word of encouragement and a reminder that God is, indeed, good. That rare gift is on full display here, offering readers comfort and reminding them of the amazing grace God offers His children.

Cal Powell

Public relations professional, Georgia

In forty years of ministry, I have heard few who so persuasively present the Word of God as Charley Chase does. In *Good, Good Father* he demonstrates this gift as he speaks to the heart about God's overflowing goodness in the life of the believer. So often our struggle is not in denying God's sovereignty but in doubting His goodness. This is especially true in the face of tragedy and disappointment. Bring your questions and your doubts to this book and allow Charley— persuasively and compassionately—to present to you the faith building case for the truth that our Father in Jesus is always up to His children's good.

Jeff Lowman
Senior Pastor, Evangel Presbyterian Church, Alabaster, Alabama

Charley Chase not only writes about the love of God, he lives his message day by day. It is an honor and privilege to sit at his feet via *Good, Good Father* and learn from one who has such a strong grasp of a truth we all need to experience, regardless of how much we have read and heard about it before.

Chip Miller
Senior Pastor, First Presbyterian Church, Macon, Georgia

Dr. Charley Chase, my beloved pastor, has a heart like the heart of Jesus, pointing us to the treasures found in enjoying God as Father. He has a winsome way of conveying rich truths, and I am so grateful for *Good, Good Father*. It is a valuable resource for any believer who desires to grow in the abundant life.

Ellen Blake
Host of A Moon in the Dark podcast
Author of *A Light Shines in Darkness*

J. I. Packer writes, 'You sum up the whole of the New Testament in a single phrase, if you speak of it as a revelation of the Fatherhood of the holy Creator. In the same way, you sum up the whole of the New Testament religion if you describe it as the knowledge of God as one's holy Father.' In *Good, Good Father* Charley Chase presses home to us the application and practice of this marvelous truth that God is our heavenly Father. Reading this book has flooded my soul with praise and adoration and makes me press toward knowing and enjoying my heavenly Father more as the Good, Good Father that He is to me in Christ.

John Owen Butler

Pastor, Lebanon Presbyterian Church, Abbeville, South Carolina

In the community where I minister there is a fatherhood epidemic. Around 80% of the children that we serve do not have a father living with them. Some of our children have never even met their earthly fathers! How desperately they—and we—need the heavenly Father! Charley's book has encouraged my heart with the wonderful assurance that God is indeed, the Good, Good Father of all who trust His Son. I pray his book will bless you the way it has blessed me!

Robin A. Crosby

Executive Director, Campus Clubs, Inc.

'Through Jesus, God is your Father.' How simple, yet profound. In other words, simply profound. In this book, with disarming sophistication, C.L. Chase carefully yet devotionally unpacks the everyday meaning of the Fatherhood of God for Christians through the appropriation of the promises of our good, good Father to His children. In addition, Dr. Chase writes with a crisp, clear, engaging style that fills the reader's mind with similes, metaphors, analogies, and bite-sized stories that both clarify the content and serve as mental speed bumps, causing the reader to slow down and savor what it means to enjoy life as a child of the ultimate Promise-Keeper.

Steve Jussely

Former Adjunct Professor of Homiletics, Reformed Theological Seminary & Senior Pastor, Lakeland Presbyterian Church, Flowood, Mississippi

GOOD, GOOD Father

Knowing *God* as He
Wants To Be *Known*

C.L. CHASE

CHRISTIAN
FOCUS

Copyright © C.L. Chase 2021

paperback ISBN 978-1-5271-0697-0
ebook ISBN 978-1-5271-0784-7

10 9 8 7 6 5 4 3 2 1

Published in 2021
by
Christian Focus Publications, Ltd.
Geanies House, Fearn,
Ross-shire, IV20 1TW, Scotland.
www.christianfocus.com

Cover design by Pete Barnsley

Printed and bound by
Bell & Bain, Glasgow

Contents

Step One:

You must immediately begin making a big deal of the truth most Christians know but fail to take seriously.

Step Two:

You must immediately begin emphasizing the Father's method of doing good to you.

Step Three:
You must immediately begin using the Father's promises to experience Fatherly good now.

In memory of Andrew James Chase and Charley Ira Chase

'… For of such is the kingdom of heaven' (Matt. 19:14).

Foreword

Her eyesight was failing; she was about eighty years old; but her hearing was acute. She greeted me after the Sunday evening service. The sermon dealt with the providence of God; memory says that the text was from Ruth. She didn't tell me I had preached a superb sermon. Her response was much better. 'Isn't God *dear?*', she exclaimed. The same tone infects this study by Charley Chase, only he expresses it a bit differently. Charley is saying, 'Isn't the Father *grand?*' He is writing to, and for, Christians and he is bill-boarding six words: Through Jesus, God is your Father. And in these meditations he unpacks what that should mean for us.

Christians in our time should welcome just this sort of book. I know we're always talking of some 'crisis' in the church (when hasn't there been one of some sort or other?) or of some dire need among Christian believers. But there are signs in some circles of the professing church that a good number don't really think that 'through Jesus, God is your Father' is so grand at all. I have been in worship settings and heard clergy address God in their prayers as 'Eternal

One,' or, 'O Holy One'—they studiously avoid calling Him 'Father.' Or you may hear something like 'Heavenly Parent,' but not 'Father.' Why this allergic reaction to God as Father? I think it's likely that they think in these times 'Father' is too 'patriarchal'—it's a relic of a male-dominant mentality that we need to leave behind. Secular culture has been preaching the gospel of gender neutrality and has begun to neuter the church's devotion. Never mind that Jesus taught us to pray, 'Our Father.' Never mind that He revealed God to us supremely as Father. No, culture must trump theology, and human preference rule divine revelation. That is not progress but poverty. Which is why it's so refreshing to have a volume like this, which sets out in such a robust and enthusiastic (can you tell?) manner all that it means for the Christian to have God as *Father*.

I would make a suggestion about reading this book. I know Dr. Chase is making a connected argument through the book, but I think you would do well to take your time reading through it. Read it a chapter at a time and let it sink in. I think especially of those chapters in Part III. What a marvelous week one would have reading and pondering one of those each day! You're likely to end up exclaiming, 'Isn't the Father *good*?'

Dr. D. Ralph Davis

Introduction: An Unknown God

Our religion is not, as someone has said, like the moon, giving light without heat, nor like the stove, giving heat without light, but like the sun, giving perennial light, and warmth, and life.—James Waddell Alexander[1]

The Bible's one-sentence biography of Jesus is 'He went about doing good.'[2] Doing good to others wasn't something Jesus did as rarely as a hanging judge shows mercy. It wasn't even something He did as frequently as a thrice-a-week golfer hits the links. It was something He did as constantly as a loving mother does each and every day with her children. Doing good to others was the way Jesus lived His life from sun-up to sundown. It was His functional DNA.

Jesus' one-sentence autobiography is, 'Whoever has seen me has seen my Father.'[3] When you look at Him you're

---

1   David B. Calhoun, *Princeton Seminary: Faith and Learning* (Edinburgh: Banner of Truth Trust, 1994), 238.

2   Acts 10:38.

3   John 14:9.

looking at a full-length, three-dimensional flesh-and-blood, live and in-person picture of God. So, putting the two sentences together, we learn that the great I AM, the true and living God, is a God who has the glorious habit of going about doing good to people.

He's especially inclined to do good to those who believe in His Son. Of them He says, 'I will not turn away from doing good to them...I will rejoice in doing them good.'[4] The Psalmist testified to God's goodness to His Old Testament people by saying, 'Truly God is good to Israel.'[5] The book of Hebrews echoes this for God's New Testament people by assuring us that He 'rewards those who seek him.'[6]

Simply put, God wants His people to know Him in the sense of *experiencing Him* in everyday life as the God who gets glory from us by doing good to us. As Paul puts it, God 'blesses us' by doing good to us so that we will 'bless' Him by lauding and loving Him.[7]

Tragically, many believers don't know Him this way. Like the Athenians, they worship an 'unknown God'[8] in the sense that they are as acquainted with the God who delights in doing them good as they are with some distant cousin they've never heard of.

This isn't saying that these believers aren't acquainted with God in the sense that they aren't Christians. Yet it was to a Christian named Philip that Jesus says, 'Have I been

---

4   Jeremiah 32:40, 41.

5   Psalm 73.1.

6   Hebrews 11:6.

7   Ephesians 1:3-14.

8   Acts 17:23.

with you so long, and you still do not know me?"[9] You can be a believer and not be acquainted with God as the God who rejoices in being good to you. I know because I was one for years.

And you can be orthodox and not be acquainted with Him as the God who enjoys being good to you. You can recite the Apostles' Creed Sunday by Sunday with the sincerity of an Apostle and yet be as unacquainted with the God who rejoices in doing good to you as Nicodemus was with the reality of the new birth[10] or a newborn child is with the names of its mom and dad. I know because I did that for years.

God doesn't want you to remain unacquainted with Him as the God whom the Apostle James winsomely describes as 'the constantly giving God.'[11] Just the opposite. He longs for you to know Him as the God who is eager to do you good things like helping you say 'No!' to temptation, answering your big prayers, continuously forgiving your sins, enabling you to conquer fear, and giving you wisdom in decision making—to inventory just a few of the items on the shelves of this wonderful grace warehouse called 'good.' In fact, He wants you to know *the single truth* about Him that assures

---

9   John 14:9.

10   John 3:4.

11   James 1:5. This is R. Kent Hughes' translation of the Greek phrase James uses. Hughes supports his translation by quoting D. Edmond Hiebert's comment on this text. Hiebert says James is stressing here that '"giving" is the inherent nature of God. The present tense of the participle sets forth God's generous nature as continually giving. He has revealed Himself as a God who is continually giving to men.' R. Kent Hughes, *James: A Faith That Works* (Wheaton, IL: Crossway Books, 1991), 282, fn. 9.

you He desires to do you these good things and many more besides. And He wants you to *understand and use the method He employs* to give them to you.

When you know this truth about God and begin using His method, you will find Him going about doing good in your life. And you will begin *consciously* giving glory to Him as you *consciously* receive good from Him.[12] This is His purpose for you. It's what Jesus means by 'abundant life.'[13]

There are three steps to knowing God as He wants to be known.

Step One: *You must immediately begin making a big deal of the truth most Christians know but fail to take seriously.*

Step Two: *You must immediately begin emphasizing the Father's method of doing good to you.*

Step Three: *You must immediately begin using the Father's promises to experience Fatherly good now.*

Here's the message of *Good, Good Father: God wants you to know Him as the Father who gets glory from you by being good to you through His promises everyday, all day long.*

By His marvelous kindness, I am getting to know Him this way.

May I introduce Him to you?

---

12   Ephesians 1:6, 12, 14.

13   John 10:10.

I

Step One to Knowing God as He Wants to Be Known:

You must immediately begin making a big deal of the truth most Christians know but fail to take seriously.

1
'I Coulda Been a Contenda!'

The fruits are normal; not to have them is not to have the Christian life which should be considered usual. There are oceans and oceans of grace which wait. Orchard upon orchard waits, vineyard upon vineyard of fruit waits. There is only one reason why they do not flow out through the Christian's life, and that is that the instrumentality of faith is not being used...we have not raised the empty hands of faith for the gift that is there.—Francis A. Schaeffer[1]

If you've never seen *On the Waterfront* put it on your bucket list. Is it that good? Absolutely!

Marlon Brando plays Terry Malloy. Rod Steiger plays Terry's older brother Charlie. Terry's an ex-boxer. Charlie's the muscle for the local mafia boss Johnny Friendly.

In an iconic scene, Terry and Charlie are riding in a cab. They're waxing nostalgic about Terry's career. Suddenly Terry hits Charlie with an unexpected verbal jab. He brings

---

1   Francis A. Schaeffer, *True Spirituality* (Wheaton, IL: Tyndale House Publishers, 1971), 83.

up a fight Charlie had him throw.[2] Charlie counters by reminding Terry they both made money on the deal. His words are a scalpel lancing a long-festering boil of bitterness in Terry's psyche. Terry oozes angst: 'You don't understand. I coulda had *class*. I coulda been a *contenda*. I coulda been a *somebody* instead of a bum…which is what I am.'

Terry's a shadow of what he could have been.

Here's good news for you: God doesn't want you to be a Terry Malloy Christian. Just the opposite. Like the old Army commercial, God wants you to 'Be all that you can be!' He sent Jesus to give you an 'abundant life.'[3]

And He wants you to live one.

Here's more good news: you can begin living abundantly **today**. Right here, right now, you can begin living a life that'll be as radical a change from what your Christian life may now be as a caterpillar's metamorphosis into a butterfly. It's as available to you as the air you breathe.

IF.

Thought so, huh? A string attached. Fine print in the contract. I can hear you saying, 'I guess you're going to tell me the same old / same old about reading my Bible more and praying more. If that's what you're selling, you need to know I've been there, done that. And, frankly, it hasn't worked for me.'

Understood. And while you can never read your Bible or pray too much, that's not the *IF* I'm talking about. The *IF* I'm talking about will surprise you as much as an unexpected Christmas bonus from a stingy boss.

---

2   A boxer 'throws' a fight when he intentionally loses it.

3   John 10:10.

'Ok, I'll bite. What's your *IF*?'

My *IF* concerns emphasizing a single truth about God. My *IF* concerns using this single truth about God more than you use any other truth. My *IF* concerns using this single truth about God as your habitat, the place where you live and move and have your being as a Christian. My *IF* concerns using this single truth about God to identify yourself, encourage yourself, calm yourself, and motivate yourself so that your Christian life is abundant instead of average or abysmal.

And my *IF* works. *If you begin using this one truth about God by making it your habitat, you'll begin living a Christian life that'll take your breath away.*

Sound too good to be true? An echo of a car salesman's exaggerated pitch or a politician's over-the-top promise or an infomercial's ludicrous claim?

I agree. My *IF* would be claiming too much if it were mine in the sense that I hold the patent on it. I don't. My *IF* isn't silk spun on the loom of my creativity.

My *IF* is HIS *IF*. It comes from God Himself.

It's God who tells you there's *one truth* that He wants you to emphasize more than any other. It's God who tells you there's *one truth* He wants you to *use* more than any other. It's God who tells you there's *one truth* He wants you to make the sun in your life's solar system. It's God who tells you there's *one truth* He wants you to think about as much as a bride thinks about her coming wedding. It's God who tells you there's *one truth* He wants you to rely on as totally as a heart patient relies on her doctor as she places herself in his hands for triple bypass surgery.

This *IF* is God's *IF*.

And it's God who tells you that *IF* you begin using this truth by making it the habitat of your Christian living you won't end up a Terry Malloy Christian. You won't end up lamenting 'I coulda been a contenda.'

Just the opposite. You'll end up living a Christian life that sings, soars, and strengthens you and causes you to give God glory for being so good to you.

Kind of makes you want to know what this one truth is doesn't it?

What's God's *IF*?

Turn the page and you'll find out.

2
God's *If*

*If you should ask me to state in one phrase what I regard as
the greatest defect in most Christian lives I would say it is our
failure to know Him as our Father as we should know Him.
That is our trouble, not difficulties about particular blessings.
The central trouble is that we do not know, as we ought to,
that God is our Father. Ah yes, we say; we do know that and
believe it. But do we know it in our daily life and living? Is
it something of which we are always conscious? If only we got
hold of this, we could smile in the face of every possibility and
eventuality that lies ahead of us.*—D. Martyn Lloyd-Jones[1]

Here's what some of the best preachers and teachers of God's
Word say about God's *IF*:

Tim Keller says God's *IF* is 'The climax of the Gospel…
Why being a Christian is a privilege…Who a Christian is…
The heart of the Christian life.'[2]

---

1   David Martyn Lloyd-Jones, *The Sermon on the Mount: Two Volumes
    in One* (Grand Rapids, MI: William B. Eerdmans Publishing Co.,
    1959) II:202.

2   Timothy Keller, *Galatians For You* (Epsom, UK: The Good Book
    Company, 2013), 89.

B. B. Warfield says God's *IF* is the demonstration of '… the high quality of the love which God bestowed on us… this great, this indescribable kind of love …'[3]

John Murray says God's *IF* is 'Surely the apex of grace and privilege…It staggers the imagination because of its amazing condescension and love.'[4]

Sinclair Ferguson says God's *IF* is 'The mainspring of Christian living…and the goal of redemption.'[5]

Gordon Fee says God's *IF* is '…the ultimate expression of grace.'[6]

J. I. Packer says God's *IF* is '…the richest answer I know to the question, "What is a Christian?"'[7]

What truth is of such importance that it takes the twenty-carat diamond language these prominent Christians use to describe it properly?

Ready?

Through Jesus, God is your Father.

Disappointed? Thought you were about to hear something astonishing, stirring, motivating? News as thrilling as being told you're about to become a first-time mom or dad? But, frankly, you're thinking, 'This isn't news at all.' You've heard it a hundred times and hearing it again is as boring as hearing

---

3   B. B. Warfield, *Faith and Life* (Edinburgh: The Banner of Truth Trust, 1974), 452.

4   John Murray, *Redemption Accomplished and Applied* (Grand Rapids, MI: William B. Eerdmans Publishing Company, 1955), 134.

5   Sinclair B. Ferguson, *Children of the Living God* (Edinburgh: The Banner of Truth Trust, 1989), 5-6.

6   Gordon D. Fee, *God's Empowering Presence* (Grand Rapids, MI: Baker Academic, 2011), 412.

7   J. I. Packer, *Knowing God* (InterVarsity Press, 1993), 200.

a Scripture song chorus sung fifteen times in a row. 'God's my Father? I know that. I thought you were going to tell me something new and exciting.'

Do that with the truth that God is your Father and you're the spiritual equivalent of a person carelessly tearing up a check for a million dollars.

Yet too many of us do act just this carelessly by treating lightly this truth that God is our Father. This explains how He's unknown to many of us. We're *acquainted* with Him as Father in the sense we're as familiar with this fact as Americans are with the Pledge of Allegiance. But we're also *unacquainted* with Him as Father in the sense that we profit from this reality as little as someone with limited computer skills profits from everything his MacBook Air can do for him.

That's tragic because profiting from the truth that God is your Father is better than having a genie offering to fulfill a hundred wishes every day of your life.

Your Father wants you to become acquainted with Him as your Father in the sense of profiting from this truth. The first way you profit from it is by treating it as He treats it. *God makes a big deal of being your Father and wants you to begin making a big deal of it, too.* Here are six assurances to encourage you.

1.

Assurance one that God makes a big deal of being your Father and wants you to begin making a big deal of it too is this: *The ultimate reason the Father sent His Son into the world is that He might become your Father too.* The ancients spoke of the Seven Wonders of the World. The seven together are as commonplace as sand in the Sahara when compared to the wonder of the Father sending His Son to live and die as 'a man of sorrows and acquainted with grief.'[8] What possessed God to do this? He tells you: 'God sent forth his Son…to redeem those who were under the law, *so that we might receive adoption as sons.*'[9]

Think of this now. God's most amazing act of grace had His becoming your Father as its final goal. Doesn't this assure you that God makes a big deal of being your Father and wants you to begin making a big deal of it too?

2.

Assurance two that God makes a big deal of being your Father and wants you to begin making a big deal of it too is this: *The ultimate reason the Father sent His Spirit to live in you is to help you live a life of delighting in Him as your Father.* I'm a jazz fan. But listening to it's an art. I need someone to

---

8   Isaiah 53:3.

9   Galatians 4:4-5. Emphasis added. Timothy Keller explains how the word 'sons' is *inclusive* rather than *exclusive*: 'Many take offense at using the masculine word "sons" to refer to all Christians, male and female…But if we are too quick to correct the biblical language, we miss the revolutionary (and radically **egalitarian**) nature of what Paul is saying. In most ancient cultures, daughters could not inherit property. Therefore, "son" meant "legal heir", which was a status forbidden to women. But the gospel tells us we are all sons of God in Christ. We are all heirs. Similarly, the Bible describes all Christians together, including men, as the "bride of Christ" (Rev. 21:2). God is evenhanded in His gender-specific metaphors. Men are part of His Son's bride, and women are His sons, His heirs. If we don't let Paul call Christian women "sons of God," we miss how radical and wonderful a claim this is.' Keller, *Galatians For You*, 90. Emphasis in original.

help me listen better. So I bought *How To Listen To Jazz* by Ted Giola. Giola's purpose in sharing his expertise is helping fans enjoy jazz more.

Similarly, living a Christian life is an art. It's the art of living a life of 'crying, Abba, Father.' Crying, Abba Father is shorthand for living every day, all day long as God's son or daughter. Our Father is so eager for us to live this way that He sends the Holy Spirit to live in us to help us: 'And because you are sons, God has sent the Spirit of his Son into our hearts, crying, "Abba, Father!"'[10]

Think of this now. Next to the gift of Jesus, God's greatest gift is the gift of the Holy Spirit. And He gives you the great gift of His Spirit so you can make much of Him being your Father. Doesn't this assure you that God makes a big deal of being your Father and wants you to begin making a big deal of it too?

3.

Assurance three that God makes a big deal of being your Father and wants you to begin making a big deal of it too is this: *The ultimate explanation of what it means for you to be Jesus' disciple emphasizes the fact that God is your Father.* West Point cadets are expected to follow a conduct manual: 'A cadet will not lie, cheat, steal, or tolerate those who do.' Jesus also has a summary conduct manual for our discipleship: the Sermon on the Mount.[11] There He tells you how He

---

10 Galatians 4:6.

11 D. Martyn Lloyd-Jones, *Studies in the Sermon on the Mount* (Mansfield Centre, CT: Martino Publishing, 2011), 17: 'This is how Christians ought to live; this is how Christians are meant to live.' John R. W. Stott says, 'The Sermon on the Mount is…the

wants you to handle big-ticket items in Christian living like dealing with those who wrong you[12], your motives,[13] use of money,[14] praying,[15] and overcoming anxiety.[16] He also gives you a multi-tasking promise to help you live His way.[17] In each case, He emphasizes the fact that you're to be governed by the truth that God is your Father.

Think of this now. According to Jesus, living as a Christian means majoring in the truth that God is your Father. Doesn't this assure you that God makes a big deal of being your Father and wants you to begin making a big deal of it too?

4.

Assurance four that God makes a big deal of being your Father and wants you to begin making a big deal of it too is this: *The ultimate way you become like Jesus is by living with God as your Father.*[18] Gatorade's 1992 commercial has

---

nearest thing to a manifesto that (Jesus) ever uttered, for it is his own description of what he wanted his followers to be and to do.' *The Message of the Sermon on the Mount* (Downers Grove, Illinois: Inter-Varsity Press, 1978), 15.

12   Matthew 5:43-48.

13   Matthew 6:1, 2-18.

14   Matthew 6:2-4; 19-24.

15   Matthew 6:5-14; 7:7-10.

16   Matthew 6:25-34.

17   Matthew 7:11.

18   In his final address John Stott eloquently proclaims that God wants us to be like Jesus: 'I remember very vividly, some years ago, that the question which perplexed me as a younger Christian (and some of my friends as well) was this: what is God's purpose for His people? Granted that we have been converted, granted that we have been

a flypaper catchy tune called 'Be Like Mike.' The 'Mike' is basketball superstar Michael Jordan. Can you be like Mike on the court? Not even if you're LeBron! But you can be like Mike by drinking his drink. You guessed it. Gatorade.

God's better than 'Be Like Mike' desire for you is: *Be like Jesus.* He wants this so much for you that it governs all of His dealings with you.[19] God's answer to every 'Why?' you ask is, 'Because I want you to be like Jesus!'

What was Jesus like? Modern physicists seek 'one unified "theory of everything."'[20] They mean one inclusive truth that explains all reality. Jesus had such a unified theory. Everything about Him is explained by the fact that His governing reality was the truth that God was His Father. Father and God are synonymous for Him. Jesus knew He was God's 'beloved Son'[21] and lived with that understanding of Himself. Not some of the time. All of the time. His

---

saved and received new life in Jesus Christ, what comes next? Of course, we knew the famous statement of the Westminster Shorter Catechism: that man's chief end is to glorify God and to enjoy Him forever: we knew that, and we believed it. We also toyed with some briefer statements, like one of only five words—love God, love your neighbor. But somehow neither of these, nor some others we could mention, seemed wholly satisfactory. So I want to share with you where my mind has come to rest as I approach the end of my pilgrimage on earth, and it is—*God wants His people to become like Christ. Christlikeness is the will of God for the people of God.'* Knowing & Doing cslewisinstitute.org, 'The Model: Becoming More Like Christ.' Emphasis added.

19 Romans 8:29; 2 Corinthians 3:18; 1 John 3:3; Philippians 3:20-21; Hebrews 12:10; 2 Peter 1:3-4.

20 Mario Livio, *Brilliant Blunders* (New York, NY: Simon & Shuster Paperbacks, 2013), 24.

21 Matthew 3:17; Matthew 17:5.

habitat was God as His *Abba, Father*. And this explains Him because it's His explanation of Himself. [22]

This means that God's supreme desire for you—that you be like Jesus—means making the fact that He is your Father the governing reality of your life—like Jesus did.

Think of this now. God's supreme desire for you—making you like Jesus—means making you someone who emphasizes His Fatherhood. Doesn't this assure you that God makes a big deal of being your Father and wants you to begin making a big deal of it too?

5.

Assurance five that God makes a big deal of being your Father and wants you to begin making a big deal of it too is this: *The ultimate expression of the magnitude of God's love for you is seen in the fact that He makes you His child.* '**What manner of** man is this?'[23] is the question coaxed from the disciples after Jesus pacified a riotous storm with a simple rebuke. They're asking, 'How do you classify Jesus?' The point is He's the only genus and species of His kind. He is the only person in existence who is fully God and fully man.

The Apostle John echoes this language of singularity as he seeks to help us understand the most loving thing God

---

22 'According to the unanimous testimony of the four gospels, Jesus *at all times*—with the sole exception of Mark 15:34 par., Matt. 24:46 which is a quotation from the Old Testament—addressed God as Father.' Joachim Jeremias, *The Prayers of Jesus* (Naperville, IL: Alec R. Allenson, Inc.1967), 108. Jeremias says Father was *the* designation Jesus used for God, calling Him this some 170 times in the gospels (19).

23 Matthew 8:27, KJV. Emphasis added.

does for us through Jesus. What's that? Become our Father: 'Behold, **what manner of** love the Father hath bestowed upon us, that we should be called the sons of God …'[24] John is telling us that the Father's act of making us His children is to His love what Jesus is to other human beings. Just as Jesus is in a class by Himself as a human being, so the Father's adopting love is in a class by itself. It's the most loving thing God does for us.[25]

Think of this now. God says 'the most loving thing I do for you through Jesus is make you my child!' Doesn't this assure you that God makes a big deal of being your Father and wants you to begin making a big deal of it too?

6.

Assurance six that God makes a big deal of being your Father and wants you to begin making a big deal of it too is this: *The ultimate truth God wants you to keep your eyes on in your hurting times is the truth that He is dealing with you as your Father.* The Puritan who said, 'God has one Son

---

24 1 John 3:1, KJV, emphasis added.

25 Jay Adam's translation and explanation of 1 John 3:1 catches the point: '**See what amazing love the Father has given to us, that we should be called the children of God—and we are!** John is so grateful for the love of God that has saved him and made him a child of God that he can hardly contain his amazement. What astounds him is God's great love. His can hardly believe that the holy God has deigned to call Himself our **Father** and us His **children.** John has written the words, but as he contemplates their meaning he can hardly believe what he has written. That is why he adds the exclamatory afterthought, **and we are!**' *The Christian Counselor's Commentary: The Gospel of John, The Letters of John and Jesus* (Woodruff, SC: Timeless Texts, 1998), 226. Emphasis in original.

without sin; He has no sons without sorrow' was right. You will have hurting times. Sometimes the hurt will be as severe as an ancient scourging. God has one ark truth He shuts you in during these flood times. One comforting, calming, cheering, contenting truth that will make you more than a conqueror: the Hebrews 12:5-13 truth that it's as your Father that He subjects you to pain. His Fatherhood assures you that your pains are grace pains: *from* Him and *for* your good.

Think of this now. The Good Samaritan truth that God sends to help you in your Jericho Road times is the truth that He is your Father. Doesn't this assure you that God makes a big deal of being your Father and wants you to begin making a big deal of it too?

7.

God's *IF* is the fact that He wants you to know Him as your Father through Jesus. *Father* is how He wants you to think of Him; *Father* is what He wants you to call Him; *Father* is how He wants you to know Him, talk to Him, live with and for Him. *All the time.* He makes a big deal of being your Father and wants you to begin making a big deal of it too. He wants you to begin taking this truth seriously.

Begin doing that.

Immediately.

It'll change your life for the better.

We'll learn how in the next chapter.

3

'When I Use a Word'

God is Father, and He alone defines what true fatherhood means.
How tragic and foolish and how very arrogant of us to shy away
from this name because some human males are poor examples of
fatherhood or because our culture regards a God named 'Father'
as oppressive and patriarchal.—Nancy Leigh DeMoss[1]

In *Through the Looking Glass* Lewis Carroll introduces us to
the smug egg named Humpty Dumpty. Humpty's a trickster
with words. He loves using them as cleverly as a magician uses
his cards. In one place in the book he's talking to the young
girl named Alice about how words are defined. In this case,
the word 'glory.' Humpty tells her that her birthday's special.
Why? Because on every other day in the year she might get
'un-birthday' presents but only on that *one* day will she get
'birthday' presents. Then he says, 'There's glory for you!'
We'll pick up the conversation from there. *Alice:* 'I don't
know what you mean by "glory."' *Humpty (contemptuously):*
'Of course you don't—till I tell you. I meant "there's a nice

---

1   gracequotes.org: Quotes about God-Fatherhood.

knock-down argument for you!"' *Alice:* 'But "glory" doesn't mean "a nice knock-down argument."' *Humpty (scornfully):* 'When I use a word it means just what I choose it to mean—neither more nor less.' *Alice:* 'The question is whether you *can* make words mean different things —that's all.' *Humpty:* 'The question is which is to be master—that's all. When I use a word it means just what I choose it to mean—neither more nor less.'[2]

Among other things, Humpty's and Alice's discussion of the meaning of words reminds us of how important definitions really are. Nowhere is this more the case than in the definition of God's Fatherhood. That's because it's what it means for God to be your Father that makes this truth of His Fatherhood so life changing. Understand what it means for you to be able to call Almighty God 'Abba, Father' and your life will become as different as the lives of parents who have just welcomed their first child into their home. Things will never be the same for them after that. And things will never be the same for you when you grasp what it means to have God as your Father.

So, how do you understand the meaning of God's Fatherhood? By paying attention to *how God uses the word 'Father.'* Father means what He says it means—neither more nor less.

1.

The prototype for understanding God's Fatherhood is NOT an earthly father. He is the *original* Father. Other fathers are, at

---

2   Lewis Carroll, *Alice's Adventures in Wonderland and Through the Looking Glass* (New York, NY: Barnes and Noble Books, 2004), 216, 218-219.

best, paternal Adams made in His image. He doesn't mirror them. They mirror Him. You don't understand what it means for Him to be a father by looking at them. You understand what it means for them to be a father by looking at Him.

Many people form their understanding of God's Fatherhood by seeing Him through the glasses of their own father. Maybe that's what you do. But doing that will, at best, make your understanding of your heavenly Father as blurry as fine print to a man needing bifocals, and, at worst, an understanding of God as wrong as the one Satan pawned off on Eve.

Say your father's a good one. A Lancelot among the knights in the paternal roundtable. When you were young you ran to him when he came home from work and jumped in his arms. Now that you're older you tell him all the time how much you appreciate him and delight in sending him thoughtful, carefully chosen Father's Day cards. Still, he'd be the first to tell you that his fatherly diamond was flawed, that he'd give a lot to be able to play a mulligan on many of his daddy decisions. The best of earthly fathers have clay feet. So, even a really, really good father can only be a snapshot of your heavenly Father, not a full-length picture. Much that's important will be left out of the frame. So, if you've had, or have, a great dad thank God for him. But don't make him the prototype for your heavenly Father. You'll make a serious mistake if you do.

You'll be even more incorrect if you've had a bad father and think of God's Fatherhood in terms of him. Some of us had/have a bad father. The kind of abusive dad writer Pat Conroy describes in his novel about his father. It's called *The Great Santini*. Conroy describes his father as a 'six feet, three inches, 230-pound Marine Corps fighter pilot' with 'knuckles dragging along the ground when he walked.' His book's first draft description of him in the person of Bull Meecham was so graphic that his editor told him 'it's simply not believable that a father would treat a son in this extraordinary way.'[3] By 'extraordinary' she meant extraordinarily bad. Conroy says he was actually light on his father because he left out the most abusive ways he was a belligerent bully. Maybe you've had your own 'Great Santini.' When you hear God described as Father it makes you nauseous. If that's you I grieve for you. And I urge you not to make your 'Santini' your prototype for Abba. You'll make a serious mistake if you do.

2.

The ONLY way to understand what it means for God to be your Father is by listening to His description of its meaning. In other words, if we're going to come under the life changing influence of being able to say, 'Abba, Father' we've got to do with God's Fatherhood what the Jews of Jesus' day had to do with their understanding of the kind of Savior God promised to send.

John the Baptist voices the Jewish expectation. Like the rest of the Jews, John expected a Rambo Messiah who would crush Rome and crown Israel King of the Nations forever. They called their expectation 'the one who is to come.'[4] Yet Jesus comes and spills no enemy blood. Jesus comes and

---

3 Pat Conroy, *A Low Country Heart: Reflections on a Writing Life* (New York, NY: Doubleday, 2016), 264, 239.

4 Matthew 11:3.

goes about doing good. Jesus comes and demands that His followers love their enemies![5]

Hearing about Jesus' dovish instead of hawkish deeds, John (now in prison for his faithfulness) sends an urgent message to Him: 'Are you the one who is to come, or shall we look for another?'[6] Jesus answers, 'Go and tell John what you hear and see: the blind receive their sight and the lame walk, lepers are cleansed and the deaf hear, and the dead are raised up, and the poor have good news preached to them.'[7]

Jesus' answer quotes Isaiah 35:5-6 and Isaiah 61:1. He's telling John, 'John, don't try to understand what it means for Me to be the Messiah from the perspective of what *people* think the Messiah should be. Understand My Messiahship from the perspective of what *God* says He's to be. Do that and you'll have the answer to your question because you'll see that I'm doing the things God sent the One to come to do.'

Jesus insists that He be understood in terms of God's description of His work rather than in terms of human expectations.

It's exactly the same with God's Fatherhood. The Father wants us to understand the meaning of His Fatherhood by *listening to His description of its meaning* not by *looking at earthly fathers and reasoning from them to Him.* His revelation, not our speculation, defines His Fatherhood.

What does God mean when He uses the word 'Father?' Christian singer/songwriter Chris Tomlin says it means that

---

5   Matthew 5:43-48.

6   Matthew 11:3.

7   Matthew 11:3-5.

God is a *Good, Good Father*: 'You're a good, good Father / It's who you are, it's who you are, it's who you are / And I'm loved by you / It's who I am, it's who I am, it's who I am.'[8]

Where did Tomlin get his definition of God? He got it from the way God uses the word 'Father.' God's definition of His Fatherhood *magnifies His love for us*[9] and *emphasizes His desire to be good to us*.[10]

3.

Christian, when you come to know God as your good, good Father your life will change for the better as surely as you experience the Lord's help when you pray. That's because your heavenly Father tells you, 'When I use the word *Father* I mean by it that I love you beyond your wildest dreams and delight in doing you all kinds of good.'

God wants you to know Him as your good, good Father. Getting to know Him this way begins with realizing how much He loves you.

We turn to His love now.

---

8   Chris Tomlin, *The Ultimate Playlist*, 2016.

9   See, for example, the connection between God's Fatherhood and His love in John 15:10, John 17:23, 1 Thessalonians 1:3-4, and 1 John 3:1.

10   See, for example, the connection between God's Fatherhood and His goodness in Matthew 7:7-11, 2 Corinthians 1:3-11, Ephesians 1:3-14, and 1 Peter 1:3-9.

4

'Ah, Me Father's So Very, Very Fond of Me'

God loves us in exactly the same way as he loved Christ. I ask again if we are able to realize that? Do you know that God in heaven at this moment loves you in exactly the same way as he loved his only begotten Son? We know his love for his Son; remember that he loves you in exactly the same way.—D. Martyn Lloyd-Jones[1]

The first thing God means by calling Himself your Father is the great truth that He loves you very much. His Fatherhood *magnifies His love for you.* And He wants you to magnify His love for you by making it the habitat of your life. The Father wants you to be like Ed Farrell's Irish uncle Seamus.

Farrell travels from Detroit to visit Seamus in Killarney on the occasion of the grand old man's eightieth birthday. When the big day arrives the men rise early, breakfast with the sunrise, then walk along the shores of Lake Killarney. The beauties of the setting awe them into twenty minutes of splendor-savoring silence. Then Seamus gets up and begins skipping along the lakeshore, smiling like a man holding

---

1   D. Martyn Lloyd-Jones, *The Assurance of Our Salvation* (Wheaton, IL: Crossway, 2000), 647.

his firstborn. Ed comes running after him, huffing like the out of shape man he is. Catching up with his uncle, he says, 'Uncle Seamus, you look so very happy. Please tell me why?' 'I am,' Seamus says, tears running down his face. 'I'm *very* happy. You see, the heavenly Father's very fond of me. Ah, me Father's so very, very fond of me!'[2]

Christian, your heavenly Father wants you to know beyond a shadow of a doubt that He is very, very fond of *you*! 'How fond?' you ask. Brace yourself for a staggering fact: *Your heavenly Father is as fond of you as He is of Jesus*! Says who? Says Jesus. Eavesdrop in adoring wonder as Jesus asks His Father to help us live in a way that makes unbelievers see that 'you sent me and *loved them even as you loved me.*'[3] Jesus Himself says that His heavenly Father, who is your heavenly Father now through Him, loves you as much as He loves Jesus!!!

This means that the Father loves you in at least the following seven ways.

1.

First, the Father loves you *eternally.* Jesus has *always* been God's 'beloved.'[4] He could say to the Father, '… you loved me before the foundation of the world.'[5] The sun of Fatherly love didn't rise on Him when He came to this earth. It always shone on Him with noonday brightness. There never

---

2   Brennan Manning, *The Wisdom of Tenderness* (New York, NY: HarperCollins Books, 2002), 25-26.

3   John 17:23. Emphasis added.

4   Ephesians 1:6. Literally, 'the one loved.'

5   John 17:24.

was a time when the Father didn't love His Son. And, dear Christian, there never was a time when He didn't love you. That's the meaning of the unusual word 'foreknew.' When Paul describes believers as those 'whom God foreknew' he's telling us that we're those whom God loved before He created the world. He makes that clear when he says that God 'in love predestined us for adoption to himself as sons through Jesus Christ.'[6] His predestining you before creation came from His pre-creation love for you. The Father has *always* loved *you* individually, you in the deep DNA sense that makes you—you.[7] Your heavenly Father loves you eternally.

---

6   Ephesians 1:4-5. John Murray writes that the Bible uses the word 'know' 'in a sense practically synonymous with "love," to set regard upon, to know with peculiar interest, delight, affection, and action.' He gives the following Scripture proofs: Genesis 18:19; Exodus 2:25; Psalm 1:6; Psalm 144:3; Jeremiah 1:5; Amos 3:2; Hosea 3:5; Matthew 7:23; 1 Corinthians 8:3; Galatians 4:9; 2 Timothy 2:19; 1 John 3:1. 'Fore' is a contraction of the word 'before.' Thus, Murray rightly explains, to be 'foreknown' by God means to be one 'whom he set regard upon' or 'whom he knew from eternity with distinguishing affection and delight' and is equivalent to 'whom he foreloved.' John Murray, *Epistle to the Romans* (Grand Rapids, MI: Wm. B. Eerdmans Publishing Co., 1959), 317.

7   The Father expresses His personal, individual love for us through Jesus. 'Jesus has done—and is still doing—so much for us that it is difficult to really believe he did all of it for each one of us personally, because he loves each of us personally. But it's true. And if we want to understand Jesus's work in saving us, then we need to get this clear and keep it clear. When Jesus created the universe; when Jesus guarded, guided, and governed his chosen people for thousands of years; when Jesus "emptied himself" and became a man; when Jesus bore years and years of servitude; when Jesus suffered under Pontius Pilate; when Jesus was crucified, dead, buried; when Jesus

2.

Second, the Father loves you *intensely*. Even the most outlandish of metaphors and most startling of similes are thimbles trying to hold the Atlantic-Ocean-immensity of the Father's love for His Son. Jesus knew He was loved with a Nebuchadnezzar's furnace hot love. His knew the Father's primary way of looking at Him was as His 'beloved Son.'[8] And His primary way of thinking about Himself and speaking about Himself was as one whom the Father loved.[9] In fact, in the parable He uses to describe His coming (the Parable of the Tenants) He describes His Father as the one who has sent servants into the vineyard looking for fruit. Finally, 'He had still one other, a beloved son. Finally he sent him to them, saying, "They will respect my son."'[10] His Father's love was so powerful, so profound, and so prevailing that Jesus defined Himself by it completely. You can do the same. The Bible uses the words 'jealousy' and 'yearning' to describe His love for you: 'Or do you suppose it is to no

---

descended to hell on the cross; when Jesus sits at the right hand of God the Father almighty, making intercession for our cause—*all this he did for you, personally. All along, as he did each and every act, he knew you completely and intimately. Each and every thing he did, he did to save you, personally.*' Greg Foster, *The Joy of Calvinism* (Wheaton, Illinois: Crossway, 2012), 49-50, emphasis added. I simply add, since Jesus reveals the Father (John 14:9) and acts for the Father (2 Cor. 5:18-19), His personal love for us expresses the Father's too.

8   Matthew 3:17; Matthew 17:5.

9   Not surprisingly, this is most clearly seen in the Gospel of John, the Apostle of love. See, for example, John 3:35; John 5:20; John10:17; John 15:9; John 17:24; John 17:26.

10 Mark 12:1-12.

purpose that the Scripture says, "He yearns jealously over the spirit that he has made to dwell in us?"'[11] Christian, the Father's love for you is reflected in the intense, jealousy-soaked yearning a right-minded husband has to be the sole object of his wife's affections. Your heavenly Father loves you intensely.

3.

Third, the Father loves you *openly.* Unlike some earthly fathers who tell their children they love them as rarely as snow falls in Miami, Jesus' Father goes out of His way to assure His Son of His love for Him. He *publically* repeats on several occasions the beautiful words, 'You are my beloved Son.'[12] He does the same with you. The cross on which the Prince of Glory dies is the supreme, undeniable affirmation of how much He loves you: 'In this is love, not that we have loved God but that he loved us and sent his Son to be the propitiation for our sins.'[13] The indwelling of the Holy Sprit is a moment-by-moment reminder that you're the object of the Father's love: '… God's love has been poured into our hearts through the Holy Spirit who has been given to us.'[14] And the very fact that the Father uses the same word to describe you that He uses to describe Jesus, shows you He loves you. The King James Version captures this truth by translating Romans 1:7, 'To all that be in Rome, *beloved of God*, called to be saints: Grace to you and peace from

---

11 James 4:5.

12 Mark 1:11; Matthew 17:5.

13 1 John 4:10.

14 Romans 5:5.

God our Father, and the Lord Jesus Christ.'[15] Your heavenly Father loves you openly.

4.

Fourth, your heavenly Father loves you *providentially.* Providence is the Oval Office word for Father's control of all His creatures and all their actions. He 'works all things according to the counsel of his will.'[16] Again, 'For from him and through him and to him are all things.'[17] Jesus rested in His Father's providence as quietly as He enjoyed REM sleep in a storm-tossed boat.[18] He rested because He knew that Fatherly providence was loving providence. In His great prayer just before He goes to the cross, Jesus summarizes His life from start to finish with three words He says to the Father: 'You loved me.'[19] Fatherly love governed Jesus' life. It governs yours too dear Christian. That's what the Father's telling you when He assures you in Romans 8:28 that He's working everything for your good.[20] Your heavenly Father loves you providentially.

---

15 Emphasis added. Compare the Greek of Romans 1:7 with the Greek of Mark 1:11. See also the KJV translation of 1 Thessalonians 1:4: 'Knowing, brethren beloved, your election of God.'

16 Ephesians 1:11.

17 Romans 11:36.

18 Matthew 8:24.

19 John 17:23, 24, 26.

20 The Westminster Confession of Faith has a soul-bracing summary of the truth that providence has a special care for believers: 'As the Providence of God doth, in general, reach to all creatures; so, after a most special manner, it taketh care of his Church, and disposeth all things to the good thereof.' Westminster Confession of Faith, 5.7. Robert Shaw writes, 'God has the interests of his own people

5.

The Father loves you *responsibly*. One of Luther's enemies taunted him by asking him where he thought he'd be when everyone turned against him. The spiritual Braveheart answered that he'd be where he'd always been: 'in the hands of almighty God.'[21] He knew that his heavenly Father lovingly took responsibility for him. He echoes his Savior in this sentiment. Jesus knew that His loving Father provided for Him, protected Him, and preserved Him for His rendezvous with the cross; enabled Him to bear the brunt of judgment for our sin; kept His body from corruption in the grave; and brought Him from the tomb to the throne.[22] The Father lovingly assumes responsibility for you too. He kept you from dying in your sins from your birth to your conversion.[23] He brought Jesus to you and you to Jesus.[24] He's provided for your material[25] and spiritual[26] needs. He's

---

ever in view; he knows what is most conducive to their happiness; and he will make all things, whether prosperous or adverse, to co-operate in promoting their good.' Robert Shaw, *The Reformed Faith* (Scotland: Christian Focus Publications, 1974 reprint), 72.

21 James S. Stewart, *Walking with God* (Edinburgh: St Andrew Press, 1996), 38.

22 A few examples among many of the Father's responsibility for Jesus' welfare are: delivering Him from Herod's infanticide (Matt. 2:13-15); preserving Him from the plots of the Pharisees to destroy Him (Luke 6:11); providing for His needs through the ministry of others (Luke 8:2-3); and keeping His dead body from decaying (Acts 2:31).

23 Romans 8:30.

24 Ephesians 1:12-14.

25 Matthew 6:25-34.

26 1 Corinthians 1:30.

keeping your eternal inheritance for you and you for it.[27] Your heavenly Father loves you responsibly.

6.

Your heavenly Father loves you *enduringly*. 'Sticktuity' was Walt Disney's self-coined word for the trait of never quitting. The Father's love for Jesus was sticktuity love. Yes, for three hours on the cross there was a spiritual eclipse. The scowling moon of His Father's wrath hid from Jesus the sunlight of His love. But though the *sense* of His love was hidden, its *reality* was still present. From the perspective of being 'made...sin'[28] for us the wrath of God was on Jesus. But from the perspective of obeying His Father by 'becoming obedient to the point of death, even death on a cross'[29] He knew 'the Father loves me because I lay down my life.'[30] The Father never stopped loving His Son. And He never stops loving you either. He continues loving you even though you disappoint, disobey, and at times defy Him. He promises you that 'neither death nor life, nor angels nor rulers, nor things present nor things to come, nor powers, nor height nor depth, nor anything else in all creation, will be able to separate us from the love of God in Christ Jesus our Lord.'[31] Your heavenly Father loves you enduringly.

---

27   1 Peter 1:1-5.

28   2 Corinthians 5:21.

29   Philippians 2:8.

30   John 10:17.

31   Romans 8:38-39.

7.

Your heavenly Father loves you *glorifying-ly.* John Calvin calls the world a 'dazzling theater' where God displays His glory by showing us how great He is.[32] Especially the greatness of His love. Paul writes that God 'works all things according to the counsel of his will.'[33] God's will is that people might 'praise the glory of his grace.'[34] His grace is His love in action. So His love is glory love in the sense that it is love determined to glorify the ones He loves. He loves Jesus with glory love because He's going to glorify Him by making every knee bow 'in heaven and on earth and under the earth and every tongue confess that Jesus Christ is Lord.'[35] And He loves you with glory love because He's going to glorify you by making you perfectly and permanently happy by making you perfectly and permanently like Jesus.[36] You will give God glory for all eternity because of His loving work of glorifying you through His dear Son.[37] Your heavenly Father loves you glorifying-ly.

8.

The undeniable evidence that the Father loves you as much as He loves Jesus is *Jesus Himself.* When Jesus wept at

---

32   John Calvin, *Institutes of the Christian Religion 1* (Philadelphia, PA: The Westminster Press, 1960), 61.

33   Ephesians 1:11.

34   Ephesians 1:6, 12, 14.

35   Philippians 2:10-11.

36   Romans 8:28-30; 1 John 3:3; Philippians 3:29.

37   Revelation 22:1-5.

Lazarus' grave people said, 'See how he loved him!'[38] When we recollect *who* Jesus is—God's beloved—consider *what* Jesus did in descending from incomparable glory to the indescribable grief of the agonies of the cross; remember *for* whom He did this, hell-deserving enemies like us; and ask *why* He did it, the unanimous answer of the New Testament is: *See how God the Father loves us!* 'In this the love of God was made manifest among us, that God sent his only Son into the world, so that we might live through him. In this is love, not that we have loved God but that he loved us and sent his Son to be the propitiation for our sins.'[39] Believer, the Savior in whom you believe is the Father's assurance that He loves you as much as He loves Jesus.

9.

One of Humphrey Bogart's most famous roles is that of Richard Blaine—aka 'Rick'—in the movie *Casablanca*. Bogie plays a man who's become a romantic cynic because the one woman he loved enough to marry suddenly and inexplicably deserted him. In a famous scene, a young woman seeks Rick's advice. She tells him she loves her husband so much she's willing to make an extraordinary sacrifice to make him happy. But she fears the sacrifice will wound her husband deeply. She asks Rick what he would do if someone loved him that much---would he forgive her? Rick's face looks like someone's just told him his best friend's died. He brushes aside the woman's question with words that groan in pain

---

38   John 11:36.

39   1 John 4:9-10.

like a mortally wounded battlefield soldier: 'No one ever loved me like that.'

Child of God, being a Christian means you're unlike Rick because you're like Seamus. Unlike Rick, you can't say 'No one ever loved me like that.' Like Seamus, you can say, 'Ah, me Father's so very, very fond of me!!!'

The question is, 'Will you take Him at His word and believe that having Him as your Father means He loves you as much as He loves Jesus?' If you will, you will begin knowing Him as your good, good Father.

5

'His Is a "Yes" Face'

Amazing grace can be a hard sell. Even today, some professing Christians find the bold message of 'Amazing Grace' tough to stomach.—Tony Reinke[1]

President Thomas Jefferson and several friends are traveling by horseback. They come to a river so swollen because of heavy rain that the only way to ford it is by horseback. A walker watches several riders make it to the other side. As Jefferson approaches the river the man asks him to ferry him across. Jefferson immediately reaches out his hand and pulls the man up behind him. They cross and the man slides off and says, 'Much obliged!' Then one of Jefferson's companions asks the man, 'What made you ask President Jefferson to do you such a favor?' 'The President?' the surprised man says. 'I didn't know that's who that is. All I know is that on some of

---

1   Tony Reinke, *Newton On The Christian Life* (Wheaton, IL: Crossway Books, 2015), 40.

your faces was the answer "No" and on some was the answer "Yes." His was a "Yes" face.'[2]

God has a 'Yes' face toward *you* Christian. He's eager to do good to *you* in your everyday living. In fact, He's set up a way for *you* to experience Him doing you good every day, all day long.

Maybe you find this as hard to believe as a no-nonsense scientist finds it to believe in UFOs. Meaning, if you're like many of us, you're saying, 'Look, I know God's been good to me in all kinds of ways. And I'm grateful. I really am. But this idea that God wants to be involved with me in the madness and messiness, the stresses and strains, the duties, difficulties, and demands of my everyday living? Give me a break. I'm not that important. Besides, He's got bigger things to concern Him.'

Fair enough. I hear you telling me that before I do anything else I need to convince you that God wants to do you good right in the middle of a job with a boss who makes Darth Vader look like a saint, a family life that's anything but 'Home, Sweet Home,' and a struggle just to get out of bed in the morning.

Ok. So, how do I convince you that God wants to do you all kinds of good smack dab in the middle of your everyday living?

I can't.

But Jesus can. Here's what He says to you. Remember, as you read this, that these are the words of the one who can no more lie than God can cease to exist: '*If you, then, who are*

---

2   Charles R. Swindoll, *The Grace Awakening* (Nashville, TN: Thomas Nelson, Inc., 2003), 4.

evil, know how to give good gifts to your children, how much more will your Father who is in heaven give good things to those who ask him![3]

Do you see what Jesus is saying to you? He's saying that God has a 'Yes' face toward you. Why? Because He's your *Father*. Now, let's begin thinking about the good the Father has for us by listening to Jesus' assurance that God's Fatherhood means God is eager to do us much good.

Jesus *gives us four guarantees that the truth that God is our Father means He is eager to do us good.*

1.

Guarantee one: Jesus says that the truth that God is our Father guarantees that good is *available* to us. 'Good gifts' and 'good things' are on the Father's agenda for us as surely as flowers, a special gift and a sumptuous meal in a fine restaurant are on a husband's for his wife on their first wedding anniversary. They're as available to us as a mother's help to her four-year-old. They await us like gifts under the tree on Christmas Day. They're ours like checks made out to us. They can be enjoyed by us as surely as the blood of Jesus can cleanse us and the Spirit of Jesus can help us. Believer, you may say with Paul that you are the 'least of all the saints', but there's good from the Father that's yours for the having.

2.

Guarantee two: Jesus says the truth that God is our Father guarantees that good is available to us *because to be a father*

---

3   Matthew 7:11.

is by definition to be a doer of good to your children.[4] The late Methodist pastor Charles L. Allen's father demonstrates this. Whenever Allen visited his father J. R.'s grave he thought of 'how good he was to me...He was happy in making us happy.'[5]

Is every father like this? No. Winston Churchill's father Randolph was a paternal nightmare. Maybe your biological dad or stepfather was/is like Randolph. Father's Day isn't your favorite holiday. That's sad to be sure. But such a 'father' is a grotesque aberration.

The truth is that most fathers, in spite of their sinfulness—what Jesus means by 'if you then being *evil*'—have Santa hearts and 'give good things to their children.' A normal father is a doer of good to his children.

In essence Jesus is saying, *If* by definition being a father means being a giver—*if*, indeed, that is so much the case that even sinful earthly fathers give their children good things—*then* 'how much more' will our perfect heavenly Father 'give good things to them that ask?'[6]

---

4   'I wish we could remember who God is when we come to Him in prayer. Sometimes we come to Him as if He were an ogre, as if He were a tyrant, an autocrat, a totalitarian despot; as if His will for our lives was paltry and mean, and He was going to cramp our style, and squash us. Our God is our heavenly Father, of infinite goodness and wisdom and kindness, and He never gives to His children anything but good.' John Stott, *John Stott at Keswick* (Colorado Springs, CO: Authentic Media, 2008), 252-253.

5   Charles L. Allen, *God's Psychiatry* (Westwood, NJ: Fleming H. Revell Co., 1953), 92-93.

6   Matthew Henry writes of this verse, 'He has assumed the relation of a Father to us, and owns us for his children...Our earthly fathers have taken care of us; we have taken care of our children; much

Christian, the very fact that God is your Father assures you that He has a giving inclination and a generous disposition toward you. He has boundless gifts available for you.

3.

Guarantee three: Jesus says the truth that God is our Father guarantees us that good is *freely* available to us. The food and drink in your childhood home didn't cost you anything did it? You ate and drank as much as you wanted and as often as you wanted without being presented a bill at the end with a 20 percent tip expected. Ditto with the Father's good things. You don't have to buy them. They've already been purchased. They're the Father's gifts through His Son.[7] They're free for the taking. The Father will 'give them' to you.

4.

Guarantee four: Jesus says the truth that God is our Father guarantees us that good gifts are *continuously* available to us.[8] God won't evict you or turn the power and water off when you don't pay the rent of walking carefully with Him and find yourself in a self-made mess. Even then He's ready

---

more will God take care of his…All the compassion of all the tender fathers in the world compared *with the tender mercies of our God*, would be but as a candle to the sun, or a drop to the ocean. God is more rich and more ready to give to his children than the fathers of our flesh can be.' *The Matthew Henry Commentary* (Grand Rapids, MI: Zondervan Publishing House, 1961), 1235.

7   Ephesians 1:3-14; 1 Timothy 6:17; James 1:17.

8   The verbs 'ask, seek, knock' in Matthew 7:7-10 are all in what we would call 'present tense' meaning continuous action.

to do you good when you 'ask him'.[9] And what's true then is true all the time. Daily, moment by moment, every day, all day long for your entire lifetime, Father's ready to give you good thing after good thing after good thing. He's *always* in a giving mood.

5.

No one less than the esteemed preacher Martyn Lloyd-Jones illustrates this truth that being a father means being a doer of good things for your children. When his daughter Elizabeth was a girl she had the hobby of collecting pictures of movie stars. The pictures came with cigarette packages. After collecting for a while, Elizabeth lacked one star: Norma Shearer. Norma's card was as elusive as a name being remembered during a senior moment. Then, at dinner after a speaking engagement, one of Lloyd-Jones' hosts pulled a packet of cigarettes out of his pocket. 'Does that package have a movie star card?' Lloyd-Jones asked. 'Yes.' 'May I see it?' 'Of course.' Guess whose card it was. You got it. Norma's! Lloyd-Jones secured the card and gave it to his daughter. Why? Because he was a father and fathers give good gifts to their children.[10]

If, as Jesus says, it's as natural as the sun giving off heat and light for an imperfect father to give good things to his children, '*how much more*' will it be the case with your perfect heavenly Father! Christian, your heavenly Father has all kinds of good things available for you.

---

9   Psalm 51; Jonah 2:1-10; 1 John 1:9.

10   Christopher Catherwood, *Chosen by God* (Winchester, IL: Crossway Books, 1986), 152-153.

Why? *Because He's your Father*!

And that guarantees that His is a 'Yes' face toward you.

The question is, will you believe Jesus' guarantees?

If you will believe them you will begin knowing God as your good, good Father.

We look next at the kinds of good the Father makes available to us.

6

'They're Included in Your Ticket'

Pleasure is a tempting thing: what yields delight, cannot but attract desire; it is next to necessity, so strongly doth it urge. Surely, if we were but fully persuaded of this, that religion hath pleasure on its side, we would be wrought upon by the allurement of that to be religious. It is certainly so, let us not be in doubt of it. Here is bait that has no hook under it, a pleasure courting you which has no pain attending to it, no bitterness at the latter end of it; a pleasure which God himself invites you to, and which will make you happy, truly and eternally happy: and shall not this work upon you?—Matthew Henry[1]

All his life he's wanted to go on a cruise. As a kid, travel brochures beckon him like an oasis enticing a parched man in the Mohave Desert. After years of Olympic athlete-like skimping on routine pleasures, he saves enough and books a passage on his dream trip. Thinking he can't afford the feast offered daily in the ship's dining room, he packs a week's supply of peanut butter, bread, and crackers. His first few days are heaven. But by midweek the peanut butter's as appetizing as an outback filet to a vegan. Desperate, he

---

1   Matthew Henry, *The Pleasantness of a Religious Life* (Fearn, Scotland: Christian Focus Publications, 1998), 45.

asks a porter, 'Please tell me how I can get a meal in the dining room. I'll do anything.' The porter answers, 'Sir, the meals are included in your ticket. You may eat as often and as much as you like.'[2]

We've seen that good things are included in the ticket of having God as our Father. It's time to see just *what* these good things are and *when* they're available.

1.

The essence of the good things the Father makes available to each of His sons and daughters is *His help in living in a way that honors and enjoys Him.* Here are *three examples* of these kinds of good things.

A.

Example one of the good things available to us is *HEART* good. A young lady asks a friend of J. I. Packer's, 'Did you ever meet C. S. Lewis?' 'Yes,' he says and adds that he's spent a good bit of time with this Hall of Fame believer. Awed, she says, 'May I touch you?'[3]

As wonderful as intimacy with Lewis would be, you have the opportunity for something infinitely better. You can have the bliss of an Enoch 'walk with God'[4] intimacy with the Father. You can have a closeness to Him that makes the best of friends seem like strangers to one another. *This is the BEST 'good thing' there is.* And the Apostle John tells you it's

---

2   John MacArthur, *Our Sufficiency in Christ* (Dallas, TX: Word Publishing, 1991), 241-242.

3   J. I. Packer, *Hot Tub Religion* (Wheaton, IL: Tyndale House Publishers, 1987), 49.

4   Genesis 5:24.

available to you when he writes, 'Our fellowship is with the Father and with his Son, Jesus Christ.'[5] Christian, *you* can have this good thing of knowing your Father well. Yes, *you* can!

B.

Example two of the good things available to us is *HALO* good. This is the good of becoming more like Jesus in our character and conduct.[6]

I will never hit a golf ball like Tiger Woods. I will never sing like Andrea Bocelli. I will never write like Ernest Hemingway. I will never coach like Coach K. I will never lead like John Maxwell. I will never act like Bogie. But I can have a pearl of great price that makes their skills seem like plastic Mardi Gras beads. I can become like Jesus. So can you.

Becoming like Jesus is what Jesus means by His well-known words, 'I came that they might have life and have it abundantly.'[7] The more like Him we are the more we will experience the things the Bible calls 'the fruit of the Spirit': 'love, joy, peace, patience, kindness, goodness, faithfulness, gentleness, self-control.'[8] These are the qualities that make life *life*. And they describe Jesus. To have *them* we must become like *Him*.

How can we be sure that the good thing of becoming more and more like Jesus is available to us? Because this

---

5   1 John 1:3.

6   2 Corinthians 3:18; Galatians 5:22-24.

7   John 10:10.

8   Galatians 5:22.

is our heavenly Father's *purpose* for us. He has 'predestined (us) to be conformed to the image of his Son.'[9] And, this is the privilege the Lord Jesus *purchased* for us through His life, death, and resurrection.[10] Then this is the Holy Spirit's *priority* for us. 'And we all, with unveiled face, beholding the glory of the Lord, are being transformed into the same image from one degree of glory to another.'[11] Whatever the Father purposes for us, the Son purchases for us, and the Spirit prioritizes for us, belongs to us.[12]

Christian, to become like Jesus is to live in the deepest sense of the word. And *you* can have this good thing of becoming more and more like Jesus. Yes, *you* can!

C.

Example three of the good things available to us is *HERO* good. This is the good of God doing for us what neither we nor anyone else can do by being our 'refuge and strength, a very present help in trouble.'[13]

The Bible showcases God's heroic deliverances of His people in ways that make comic book heroes like Superman, Batman, and Wonder Woman seem stick figure impotent

---

9   Romans 8:29.

10   Titus 2:14; Hebrews 9:12. Jesus 'purchased' us by redeeming us. Redemption in the New Testament involves 'the idea of release by payment.' Leon Morris, *The Apostolic Preaching of the Cross* (Grand Rapids, MI: Wm. B. Eerdmans Publishing Co., 1955), 12. The price He paid was that of 'bearing what we should have born,' viz., the curse of God, Galatians 3:13. Ibid. 61.

11   2 Corinthians 3:18.

12   'For all things are yours,' 1 Corinthians 3:21.

13   Psalm 46:1.

by comparison. For example, His exploits in the lives of Abraham, Joseph, David, Daniel, Shadrach, Meshach, Abednego, Paul, and, supremely, the Lord Jesus Christ make all these superheroes seem tame by comparison.[14]

We read these stories and think, 'What a mighty God we serve!' And we wish these biographies could be ours. The Bible assures us they can by telling us 'Whatever was written in former days was written *for our instruction*, that through endurance and through the encouragement of the Scriptures we might have hope.'[15]

Christian, *you* can have this good thing of experiencing Father at His best when your life is at its worse. You can experience Him delivering you from temptations, sustaining you in difficulties, and guiding you in critical decision-making moments—to mention just a few of the heroics the Father's willing to engage in with you. Yes, *you* can!

2.

These heart, halo, and hero blessings are available to you *EVERYWHERE and ALL THE TIME*. They were available to Joseph in Mrs. Potiphar's house, Moses at the Red Sea, Elijah in a drought, Nehemiah in a pagan palace, Daniel in a lion's den, Paul in jail, and the Lord Jesus on the cross.[16] They're

---

14 Genesis 12-25:11 (Abraham); Genesis 39:6-12 (Joseph); Exodus 14:21-31 (Moses); 1 Kings 17:1-16 (Elijah); Nehemiah 2:1-8 (Nehemiah); Daniel 3:19-30 (Shadrach, Meshach & Abednego); 2 Timothy 4:16-18 (Paul); Psalm 22 (Jesus).

15 Romans 15:4, emphasis added.

16 Genesis 39:10 (Abraham); Exodus 12:15-19 (Moses); Nehemiah 2:4 (Nehemiah); Daniel 6:16-24 (Daniel); Philippians 1:12-18 (Paul); John 16:32 (Jesus).

available to you in a business meeting, sorority / fraternity house, and LA freeway-heavy traffic; on an operating room table, a football field, and in a dentist's chair; in your good times and bad; your ordinary days and extraordinary days. When the Psalmist says, 'If I take the wings of the morning and dwell in the uttermost parts of the sea, even there your hand shall lead me, and your right hand shall hold me'[17] he's assuring us that *wherever we are* the Father is willing to do good things for us.

Like emergency room doctors with an attempted suicide, good things are *even available when we're bleeding from self-inflicted wounds*. In those times we'll find what disobedient Jonah found sinking to the bottom of the ocean, foolish Jehoshaphat found in a battle he had no business fighting, and proud Peter found while aching with excruciating guilt for denying Jesus.[18] Like them, we'll find in these times the good thing 'that neither death nor life, nor angels nor rulers, nor things present nor things to come, nor powers, nor height nor depth, nor anything else in all creation will be able to separate us from the love of God in Christ Jesus our Lord.'[19]

3.

Prosperity gospel preachers are *right and wrong*. They are right when they assure us Father wants us healthy and wealthy. But they're wrong when they tell us the wealth He

---

17 Psalm 139:9-10.

18 Jonah 2:1-10; 1 Kings 22:32; John 21:15-19.

19 Romans 8:38-39.

wants for us is Bill Gates-like finances and the health He wants for us is triathlete-like fitness.

The health and wealth our Father wants for us is made up of *spiritual* good things. Their essence is God Himself because they *come* from Him and *consist* of His Fatherly goodness in Jesus. You can say of them what Anglican preacher and poet George Herbert says of the sacraments: they 'bring my God to me.'[20]

This is what makes them the very best things our Father can do for us. Nothing compares to them.

And they're *all* included in *your* ticket of having God as your Father.

Best of all, He wants *you* to begin enjoying them *now* because this is what it means for Him to be your good, good Father.

He wants you to know Him this way because it's the way He'll get glory from you in your everyday living.

We look at this in the next chapter.

---

20 George Herbert, *The Country Parson, The Temple* (NJ: Paulist Press, 1981), xiv.

7

'A Gift! Delight it; DELIGHT it!'

There is a kind of eagerness about the beneficence of God. He does not wait for us to come to him. He seeks us out, because it is his pleasure to do us good. 'The eyes of the Lord run to and fro throughout the whole earth, to show his might in behalf of those whose heart is whole toward him' (2 Chronicles 16:9). God is not waiting for us; he is pursuing us. That, in fact, is the literal translation of Psalm 23:6: 'Surely goodness and mercy shall pursue me all the days of my life.' I have never forgotten how a great teacher once explained it to me. He said God is like a highway patrolman pursuing you down the interstate with lights flashing and siren blaring to get you to stop—not to give you a ticket, but to give you a message so good it couldn't wait until you got home.—John Piper[1]

Michael Yankoski joins a friend and his family on a two-week vacation to Paris. After a week in a cramped flat, Yankoski is stir crazy. So, at 5.30 one morning he begins a solo exploration of the city. He's enjoying himself until

---

1   John Piper, *The Pleasures of God* (Portland, OR: Multnomah, 1991), 191.

a menacing voice from behind wakes him to the fact he's wandered into a dark part of the City of Lights. Michael turns and sees three black-hooded men who obviously aren't from the Paris Tourist Board. He takes off with them following. Turning into a cul-de-sac, Yankoski fears he's about to become a crime statistic. But seeing an open back door and a flour-dusted baker taking a cigarette break he runs toward him shouting, 'Help!' Seeing the pursuers, the baker escorts Yankoski inside and locks the door. A few minutes later, he offers him a fresh baguette. Yankoski pats his pockets: 'No money!' The baker says, 'No, no. A gift, a *gift*! For your trouble.' He then escorts Michael to the front door, checks to make sure it's safe outside, and bids him 'au revoir.' Outside, Yankoski thanks him. The smiling baker says, 'A gift! Delight it, *delight* it.'[2]

Gifts are given to be enjoyed. By givers like this baker. Best of all, by the best of givers, our heavenly Father. His baguettes are all the good gifts He makes available to us now. And He wants us to enjoy them every day, all day long.

We can put it this way: *Father wants you to know Him as the God who gets glory from you by giving you good gifts to enjoy.*

Psalm 34:8 says: 'Oh, taste and see that the Lord is good!'

1.

Father wants us to *enjoy good gifts*. Dr. Martyn Lloyd-Jones is right when he tells us 'We are meant to enjoy the Christian

---

2   Michael Yankoski, *The Sacred Year* (Nashville, TN: W Publishing, 2014), 50-51.

life.'[3] That's what the Psalmist means when he tells us to 'taste' that the Lord is good. Tasting means *enjoying*. We bite into a McDonald's french fry and *enjoy* its salty hot crunchiness. We sip our morning cup of steaming java and *enjoy* its awakening, bittersweet blend of coffee, cream, and sugar. We sink our teeth into a Milky Way candy bar and *enjoy* the singular deliciousness of chocolate, caramel, and nougat. Similarly, tasting that the Lord is good means *enjoying* His goodness. And one of the ways we do this is by *enjoying* Him doing us good in our everyday living.

2.

It's *Father Himself* who wants us to enjoy Him being good to us. He's the One telling us 'taste and see that the Lord is good.' We need to know this because as far back as Eden, Satan broadcast the false news that Father and enjoyment are antonyms. He's still spreading this lie. And, truth be told, many of us harbor a sneaking suspicion that the devil's right, that Father is a 'hard man,'[4] as stern and aloof as a Victorian father. Yet here Father Himself rings the dinner bell and urges us to eat from the table of His goodness with the heartiness of lumberjacks after a long day in the woods and the fearlessness of children whose metabolism's the best weight watcher program there is. Maybe the first good thing you need to enjoy is this truth that it's Father Himself who wants you to taste and see that the Lord is good. If so, 'Bon Appetit'!

---

3   D. M. Lloyd-Jones, *Romans: The Final Perseverance of the Saints* (Grand Rapids, MI: Zondervan Publishing House, 1976), 96.

4   Matthew 25:24.

3.

Father wants *each* of us to enjoy Him being good to us.[5] Enjoying Him this way isn't the spiritual equivalent of a country club membership that's available only to a select few. They're like the manna the Lord gave Israel in the wilderness. He told them, 'Gather of it, *each one of you*, as much as he can eat.'[6] Father says of His good things what Jesus says of the cup at the Supper, 'Drink of it, *all of you*.'[7] Just as a mother wants every one of her children to be healthy and a shepherd wants every sheep in his flock to be safe and a general wants every soldier under his command to come back from battle alive, so Father wants every one of His sons and daughters to experience His goodness in their everyday living. Christian, He wants *you* to taste and see that the Lord is good.

4.

Father wants each of us to enjoy *every* good He is willing to do us.[8] There was one tree in Eden that Adam and Eve were to avoid as though it was laced with arsenic.[9] There isn't a single tree in the garden of His good things that's off our diet. That's because not one of them is bad for you. No gluten,

---

5   Psalm 34:9 makes this clear by emphasizing that it's 'You his saints,' i.e., all His people, that are invited to enjoy the Lord's goodness.

6   Exodus 16:16. Emphasis added.

7   Matthew 26:27. Emphasis added.

8   1 Corinthians 3:21; 2 Peter 1:4.

9   Genesis 2:16-17: 'And the Lord God commanded the man, saying, "You may surely eat of every tree of the garden, but of the tree of the knowledge of good and evil you shall not eat, for in the day that you eat of it you shall surely die."'

refined sugar, high fructose, or high omega-6 fats either. No
junk food. No chemically-processed meat, cheese, or bread.
No preservatives that keep food from spoiling while spoiling
your health if you eat them. Better still, you can devour
these blessings like a chocaholic eating a pound of M&M's
and you won't gain a pound, raise your bad cholesterol, clog
up your arteries, or increase your risk of cancer. Every good
gift your Father gives you is better for your soul than fruits,
vegetables, and water are for your body. Every one of them
is available to you every day all day long. And your Father
wants you to enjoy every one of them.

5.

Father wants us to enjoy Him doing us good in our
everyday living because this *glorifies* Him. The mercies of
His heart, halo, and hero good produce HALLELUJAH
glory. Enjoying these good things will delight us better than
our best Christmas ever; calm us in a manner that makes
Xanax seem like an energy drink; and empower us the way
love empowers a mother to sacrifice for her children. And
enjoying them makes us 'rich toward God'[10] with a wealth
that makes Amazon's Jeff Bezos look like a pauper and a
health that makes the physically fittest human on the planet
seem like someone in the final stages of a terminal illness.
Because of this, experiencing the Father's goodness leads to
that delight in Him that'll make you say with the Psalmist,
'Praise the Lord! Oh, give thanks to the Lord, for he is good'
and that devotion to Him that makes you present your body

---

10 Luke 12:21.

'as a living sacrifice' in trust, obedience, and endurance.[11] Simply put, the more you enjoy your Father's goodness the more you'll glorify Him. Since this is what He most wants, you can rest assured that He wants you to enjoy Him doing you good every day, all day long.

6.

Father wants you to be a Grace-Focused Optimist about His desire to do you good. He wants you to be *optimistic* that He is your Father and that as your Father He delights in being good to you (=*grace*) every day, all day long by helping you honor and enjoy Him. He wants you to *focus* on this truth and build your life on it.

When you become a Grace-Focused Optimist about Father's zeal to be good to you by:

- Making as big a deal of the truth that He is your Father as He does
- Embracing the fact that He delights in doing you great good
- Longing to enjoy His goodness every day all day long

Then you are listening to Him as He tells you that His goodness is 'A Gift' and that He wants you to 'Delight it! *Delight it!*'

When you reach this point you've taken Step One in becoming acquainted with the Father who delights in getting glory from you by being good to you.

And the unknown God will be the known God as you now know Him as the good, good Father that He is.

---

11   Psalm 106:1; Romans 12:1.

Take Step One now! From this moment on, begin making a big deal of the truth that God is your Father and this means He delights in showing His goodness to you. From this moment on, think of God as your Father. From this moment on, speak to God as your Father. And from this moment on, glorify God as your Father by tasting and seeing that the Lord is good.

7.

To enjoy the good the Father wants to do you every day, all day long, you must understand *how* He engages in doing you good.

Step Two tells you how.

We turn there now.

2

Step Two to Knowing God as He Wants to Be Known:

You must immediately begin emphasizing the Father's method of doing good to you.

8

The Father's M.O.

Take the promises of God. Let a man feed for a month on the promises of God, and he will not talk about how poor he is... If you would only read from Genesis to Revelation and see the promises made by God to Abraham, to Isaac, to Jacob, to the Jews and to the Gentiles, and to all His people everywhere—if you spend a month feeding on the precious promises of God— you wouldn't be going about complaining how poor you are. You would lift up your head and proclaim the riches of His Grace, because you couldn't help doing it.—D. L. Moody[1]

A group of ministers is extolling Dr. Martyn Lloyd-Jones. He's not present but his wife is. Their oral applause centers on Lloyd-Jones' remarkable abilities. While appreciating the things being said, Mrs. Lloyd-Jones thinks everyone is missing what makes her husband tick. Quietly she says, 'No one will ever understand my husband until they realize that he is first of all a man of prayer and then, an evangelist.'[2] According to the person who knew him best, prayer and

---

1   Herbert Lockyer, *All the Promises of the Bible* (Grand Rapids, MI: Zondervan, 1962), 6.

2   D. M. Lloyd-Jones, *Old Testament Evangelistic Sermons* (Edinburgh: The Banner of Truth Trust, 1995), vii.

evangelizing were Lloyd-Jones' M.O. (his method of operating).

Similarly, we'll never understand our Father and enjoy the blessings He makes available unless we realize that His M.O. for giving them to us *prioritizes* something most Christians minimize. Frankly, unless you're a believer who's an ant at the literary picnics of writers like Charles H. Spurgeon, the Puritans, J. C. Ryle, and their modern cousins like John Piper and Joel Beeke; *and/or* you have the privilege of eating fruit from a pulpit ministry that's a tree planted by a river of men like these, you've probably heard very little about God's M.O. for doing good to His people.

What do older writers and preachers and a few modern ones emphasize that many (most?) of today's writers and preachers don't even mention?

Ready?

Father's PROMISES to us.

Older writers and preachers trumpet Father's promises as His M.O. for doing us good. And they do this because the Bible does. The illustrious Mr. Spurgeon crisply captures the Bible's emphasis on the promises as the Father's M.O. for working graciously in our lives in the title he gives his book on the Lord's promises: *According to Promise or The Lord's Method of Dealing with His Chosen People.*[3]

I ask you: doesn't this surprise you the way being stopped by a highway patrolman for speeding and getting off with only a warning would? When's the last time you heard a sermon on the importance of using Father's promises to bless you as daily, routinely and expectantly as you use cash

---

3   Ichthus Publications Edition, 2014.

and credit cards to pay bills and shop and eat and gas up your car? More to the point, when's the last time you *enjoyed* a specific good by *intentionally* using a promise? If you're like most Christians, probably as recently as the last time you used a rotary phone.

It's this neglect of Father's promises that explains why we aren't enjoying available good like a child enjoying a swimming pool on a hot August day in Atlanta. Please hear this. It's not our quiet time inconsistency or our sometimes disobedience or Father's reluctance to be good to us that leaves us feeling deprived of much of His goodness. The sole reason we aren't enjoying more of His gracious activity in our lives is that we're not using His promises every day, all day long. Expecting to experience available good while neglecting His promises is the equivalent of refusing to drink water yet expecting to stay hydrated. It's not going to happen.

The preacher William Jay says preachers ought to use words that 'strike and stick.' *Strike*, in the sense of arresting attention; *stick*, in the sense of giving people something to take with them. Here's my strike and stick about you and Father's promises: Father wants you to become a promise addict. He wants His promises to be to you what a drug is to a junkie in the sense that you become so dependent on them that you can't live a day without them.

Got your attention? Good. Because Father's M.O. for being good to you is through His promises. So, how do you begin mainlining them? *You must embed in yourself the habit of using Father's promises as a grace-focused optimist every day, all day long.* Father's M.O. must become your M.O. too.

The place to begin embedding this habit is by realizing that the former generations were right in making a big deal of Father's promises because they really are His M.O. for being good to us.

We turn to this now.

9

A Big Message From Two Little Words

God relates to his children largely through promises.—
Richard Philips[1]

A Sunday school teacher asks her fourth graders 'Does anyone
know the meaning of the word "precious"?' A boy's hand
shoots up, his smiling face broadcasting 'I do!' confidence.
'Yes, Billy, what does "precious" mean?' '"Precious" means
"whatever would we do without her?"' 'Billy, that's wonderful.
Where'd you get such a sweet definition?' 'From Daddy. He
calls mommy "precious" because he says "Whatever would
we do without her?"' Out of the mouths of babes, huh?

Two little words give us the big message that Father's
promises are 'Whatever would we do without them?'
precious and indispensable to our enjoying His help every
day, all day long. The words are '*through them*.' Peter
writes, Father 'has granted to us his precious and very great
promises so that *through them* you may become partakers of

---

1   Richard Philips, *Faith Victorious* (Phillipsburg, NJ: P&R Publishing
     Company, 2002), 81.

the divine nature, having escaped from the corruption that is in the world because of sinful desire.'[2]

The big message of these two little words is this truth: *You begin enjoying the good the Father wants to do you as a Grace-Focused Optimist by realizing that Father's way of giving them to you is through His promises.*

He gives His promises a starring role in His Grace Story. He wants you to give them the same role in your chapter (your life) in that Story.

Here are ten of many biblical examples of the truth that Father's way of giving good gifts is through His promises.

Father gives the good gift of comfort through a paramedic promise to Adam and Eve as they lie bleeding with internal and external injuries from their head-on collision with sin by promising to curse the serpent: 'I will put enmity between you and the woman, and between your offspring and her offspring; he shall bruise your head, and you shall bruise his heel.'[3] *Through them*, you see.

Father gives the good gift of spiritual wealth through a portfolio of bull market promises to Abraham: 'Now the Lord said to Abram, "Go from your country and your kindred and your father's house to the land that I will show you. And I will make of you a great nation, and I will bless you and make your name great, so that you will be a blessing. I will bless those who bless you, and him who dishonors you I will curse, and in you all the families of the earth shall be blessed."'[4] *Through them*, you see.

---

2   2 Peter 1:4.

3   Genesis 3:15.

4   Genesis 12:1-3.

Father gives the good gift of rescue from their Egyptian hostage situation through a SWAT team promise to Israel: 'Then the Lord said to Abram, "Know for certain that your offspring will be sojourners in a land that is not theirs and will be servants there, and they will be afflicted for four hundred years. But I will bring judgment on the nation that they serve, and afterward they shall come out with great possessions."'5 *Through them*, you see.

Father gives the good gift of victory in the battle for the promised land through an invincible ally promise to Joshua: 'No man shall be able to stand before you all the days of your life. Just as I was with Moses, so I will be with you. I will not leave you or forsake you. Be strong and courageous, for you shall cause this people to inherit the land that I swore to their fathers to give them.'6 *Through them*, you see.

Father gives the good gift of healing from a terminal disease through a wonder drug promise to give fifteen more years to King Hezekiah: 'Then the word of the Lord came to Isaiah: "Go and say to Hezekiah, Thus says the Lord, the God of David your father: I have heard your prayer; I have seen your tears. Behold, I will add fifteen years to your life."'7 *Through them*, you see.

Father gives the good gift of being the mother of the Messiah through a stork promise to a young Jewish teenager named Mary: 'And the angel said to her, "Do not be afraid, Mary, for you have found favor with God. And behold, you

---

5   Genesis 15:13-14.

6   Joshua 1:4-5.

7   Isaiah 38:5.

will conceive in your womb and bear a son, and you shall call his name Jesus.'''[8] *Through them*, you see.

Father gives the good gift of guarding Peter's faith from Satan's assassination attempt through a bodyguard promise Jesus makes to him: 'Simon, Simon, behold, Satan demanded to have you, that he might sift you like wheat, but I have prayed for you that your faith may not fail. And when you have turned again, strengthen your brothers.'[9] *Through them*, you see.

Father gives the good gift of making every believer's heart the Spirit's dwelling by a grace temple promise to Jesus: 'This Jesus God raised up, and of that we are all witnesses. Being therefore exalted at the right hand of God, and having received from the Father the promise of the Holy Spirit, he has poured out this that you yourselves are seeing and hearing.'[10] *Through them*, you see.

Father gives the good gift of rescuing 276 people from drowning in a storm through a lifeguard promise to passenger Paul: 'For this very night there stood before me an angel of the God to whom I belong and whom I worship, and he said, "Do not be afraid, Paul; you must stand before Caesar. And behold, God has granted you all those who sail with you." So take heart, men, for I have faith in God that it will be exactly as I have been told.'[11] *Through them*, you see.

Father gives the good gift of consolation in the worst of pains through a panacea promise to each of His people:

---

8   Luke 1:30-31.

9   Luke 22:31-32.

10   Acts 2:32-33.

11   Acts 27:23-25.

'And we know that for those who love God all things work together for good, for those who are called according to his purpose.'[12] *Through them*, you see.

Are you getting the big message from the two little words 'through them'? Father's M.O. for giving good gifts *to* you is *through* His promises.

His M.O. must become yours.

You must begin treating His promises for what they are. What's that? Precious. Why? Because whatever would you do without them?

Still, understanding that Father's M.O. for being good to you is through His promises won't help you use them unless you understand what a promise from Father is.

What is Father doing when He makes you a promise?

We look at this next.

---

12 Romans 8:28.

10

God Has Given Me Some Promises

The heroes in the Bible came from all walks of life: rulers, servants, teachers, doctors. They were male, female, single, and married. Yet one common denominator united them: they built their lives on the promises of God...The question is not, will God keep his promises, but, will we build our lives upon them?—Max Lucado[1]

Imagine something.

Imagine that the owner of an entire grocery store chain calls you. Addressing you warmly, he tells you your name's been picked in a random draw. You'd forgotten you'd entered—after all, you never win anything. But now you have. And the big boss is happy to tell you you've won a lifetime of free shopping at any of his stores. 'Whatever's on the shelves is yours,' he says. 'As much as you want. Whenever you want. 24/7, 365, for the rest of your life. We're sending you a free and unlimited shopping card. It'll always be honored at any of our stores. Use it as often as you wish.'

---

1   Max Lucado, *Unshakeable Hope* (Nashville, TN: Thomas Nelsen, 2018), 4, 8.

What would you do? You'd start using that card wouldn't you? Gladly, regularly, and boldly you'd begin walking into any of their stores in the country to use your card to get whatever you want whenever you want it.

Guess what?

You have something even better. You can say what the late Dawson Trotman said: 'God has given me some promises that I know He will fulfill.'[2] By giving you His promises Father's giving you something infinitely superior to an unlimited grocery card. When you understand what a promise from Him is you'll see why this is the case.

What is Father doing when He gives you a promise? *When Father makes you a promise He's specifying an individual good thing He's always ready to do for you.*

Here are six facts about His promises that make them the incomparable gifts that they are.

1.

Father's promises *specify specific good things He's willing to do for you now.* Stand by the candy shelves in a convenience store. You'll find a variety of yummy choices. Each in its own wrapper telling you *exactly* what sugary pleasure it's offering you: Junior Mints or Snickers or M&M's...

Father's promises do something similar. Grace is Father saying to you what He says to Jacob: 'I will surely do you good.'[3] Meaning, among other things, 'I have good things I will gladly do you.' An individual promise is Father's way of

---

2   Thomas R. Yeakley, *Praying Over God's Promises* (Colorado Springs, CO: NavPress, 1994), 37.

3   Genesis 32:12.

telling you *exactly* what good He's offering to do for you. So, for example, the promise in 1 John 1:9 offers you the specific good of 'forgiveness'; the promise in James 1:5 offers you the specific good of 'wisdom'; the promise in Isaiah 40:31 offers you the specific good of 'renewed strength'; the promise in John 14:27 offers you the specific good of 'peace'; and, the promise in Philippians 4:19 offers you the specific good of the 'supply of every need.' Each promise identifies a specific good Father is ready to do for you.

2.

Father's promises are *yours*. They aren't form letters addressed to 'Occupant.' They're sent to your mailbox with your name on them. Peter says Father has granted His promises 'to us.'[4] He identifies 'us' as 'those who have obtained a faith of equal standing with ours by the righteousness of our God and Savior Jesus Christ.'[5] In other words, believers. That's you isn't it? So, Father's promises are yours. He makes His promises to you![6]

---

4   2 Peter 1:4.

5   2 Peter 1:1.

6   *Charles Spurgeon* says the promises 'are not allotments hedged in for individuals, but they are a wide and open common, which is **the undisputed property of all believers**. They are not confined to those to whom they were first spoken, but they reach also to us who are fellow heirs with them' The Metropolitan Tabernacle Pulpit, Volume 33, page 5. Emphasis added. 2 Corinthians 1:20 says, 'For all the promises of God find their Yes in him. That is why it is through him that we utter our Amen to God for his glory.' John Piper argues that this '**means that in union with Christ, the Messiah, Christians become the heirs of all the promises in the Old Testament…Christians are Messianic people, the true**

3.

Father makes you *numerous* promises. Peter tells you they're 'great.'[7] They're certainly great in number. Father hasn't given you just a few promises, scattering them here and there like rare compliments from a demanding teacher. Just the opposite. The Bible's crowded with promises. It's a sky full of promise stars; a bank full of promise cash; a Fort Knox full of promise gold; a Garden of Eden full of promise trees that are pleasant to the sight and good for food; a chocolate box of treats. Father offers you lots and lots of good things.[8]

4.

Father makes you *stupendous* promises. Christians are often challenged to pray God-sized prayers: prayers so big that

---

Israel, the heirs of everything promised to the true Israel.' He argues similarly from 2 Corinthians 3:21-22. Emphasis added. http://www.desiringgod.org/interviews/which-old-testament-promises-apply. The Bible makes clear that all of the promises are yours by urging you to claim promises made to people in Scripture. Take a couple of examples. In Romans 16:20 Paul sharpens our sword for fighting sin on the whetstone of God's promise in Genesis 3:15 to Adam and Eve about defeating Satan. Hebrews 13:5-6 tells you to endorse and cash for yourself the promise check God writes Joshua in Joshua 1:5. And Peter customizes Jesus' promise to him in Luke 22:32 and uses it to encourage in 1 Peter 1:5 the persecuted Christians to whom he writes with the assurance that God's power will be their faith's bodyguard against Satan's attempts to assassinate it. Again and again throughout Scripture, the promises are used as the community property of every Christian. This means that as a member of this community the promises are yours.

7   2 Peter 1:4.

8   Estimates of the number of promises God makes in the Bible range from approximately 3,500 to over 7,000.

only God can answer them. Father makes Father-sized promises: promises so big that only a Father as big (and good!) as He is can keep them. He promises you 'all things that pertain to life and godliness.'[9] Whatever you need to live abundantly and die triumphantly is available to you through His promises. From veteran warrior promises always volunteering for front line duty to 5-Hour Energy drink promises capable of stimulating you to action to Good Samaritan promises able to care for you when you're mugged on life's Jericho Road, Father's promises are nothing less than Father Himself telling you of ways that He is able and willing to do for us 'far more abundantly than all that we ask or think.'[10]

5.

Father makes you *suitable* promises. As a Christian, you're like a fabulously wealthy man with a house full of servants. He has a servant for everything. A servant to cook his meals; a servant to chauffeur his car; a servant to draw his bath; a servant to lay out his clothes; a servant to answer his door. Just so with you. Father's promises help you 'become' a partaker 'of the divine nature.'[11] This means there's a promise to help you be like Jesus wherever you are, whatever you're doing. There's always a promise offering you exactly the help you need at any given moment. There's a promise tool for every job; promise clothing for every occasion; and promise medication for every ailment. You never swim in waters

---

9   2 Peter 1:3.

10   Ephesians 3:20.

11   2 Peter 1:3-4.

without a lifeguard promise ready to rescue you. You never walk dark streets in bad neighborhoods without a police promise to escort you. You never fight a battle without a soldier promise with you in your foxhole.[12]

6.

Father makes you *effective* promises. He offers oasis not mirage help. Field-tested weapons for real soldiers engaged in real battles. NFL first draft choices that not only look good on paper but also become all-pro performers. The ability of the promises that made Abraham ready to offer Isaac, Moses able to face Pharaoh, David courageous before Goliath, Solomon savvy enough to cut a Gordian knot, Mary calm before the possibility of becoming a pariah to Joseph and their families and friends, and our blessed Lord Jesus ready to walk the Via Dolorosa, stands behind every promise Father's made you.[13]

---

12 Charles Simeon writes, 'God's promises comprehend everything which our necessities require. Place us in any situation imaginable, and there will be found a promise directly applicable to our state.' *Expository Outlines on the Whole Bible*, Vol. 20 (Grand Rapids, MI: Baker Books, 1988), 287. William Bridge writes, 'God has promises of comfort, succor, and relief, suitable to all conditions. I dare boldly challenge all men to show me any one condition for which God has not provided a promise of comfort, mercy, and succor suitable unto it.' William Bridge B/T, August 13, 2014. Jerry Bridges writes, 'There is not a single situation that arises in your life for which there is not a promise from God that will address that situation.'

13 Genesis 22:1-19 (Abraham); Exodus 3:1-22 (Moses); 1 Samuel 17:20-54 (David); 1 Kings 3:16-28 (Solomon); Luke 1:34-38 (Mary); John 19:11 (Jesus).

Put another way, His promises will accomplish their purpose of helping you become a partaker of the divine nature. The forgiveness He offers you by promise removes your guilt as far as the east is from the west. The wisdom He offers you by promise will make you Solomon-smart. The strength He offers you by promise will make you Samson-strong. The peace He offers you by promise will make you calm as a Norman Rockwell painting. No promise comes with a money back guarantee. It doesn't need one. You'll never regret using any of Father's promises. You'll never find a single one disappointing you.

7.

Doesn't this truth that God has given you some promises make you better off than you'd be with an unlimited spending card for groceries?

Maybe you're thinking 'This sounds too good to be true.' Is it? Is this making Father's promises bite off more than they can chew? After all, ordinary as you are, He nonetheless makes you some extraordinary promises. Can you take seriously such big promises given to someone as small as you?

A single truth about Father's promises says, 'Yes, you can!' We look at this truth now.

11
Infallible Predictions

Though God dwells in the center of eternal mystery, there need be no uncertainty about how He will act in any situation covered by His promises. These promises are infallible predictions. God will always do what He has promised to do when His conditions are met... —A.W. Tozer[1]

Every promise Father makes you is as much an infallible prediction as an Old Testament prophecy. It's a *prediction* in the sense that it tells you something Father is going to do just as those prophecies crystal-balled His future actions. And it's *infallible* in the sense that each promise is as sure to be kept as the prophecies were to be fulfilled. Father can no more fail to keep a promise than He can cease being I AM.[2]

Nothing encourages you to begin using Father's promises like this assurance that every promise is as sure to be kept as Jesus is to return. Here's our truth for now: *Father wants*

---

1   Thomas R. Yeakley, *Praying Over God's Promises: The Lost Art of Taking Him at His Word* (Colorado Springs, CO: NavPress, 1994), 71.

2   Joshua 24:13; 2 Corinthians 1:19-20.

you to use His promises because He has the will and skill to keep every promise He makes.

Here are three assurances out of many that Father keeps His promises.

1.

Assurance one that Father will keep His promises is the fact *His glory depends on keeping every one of them.* His glory, in the sense of His reputation as the Supreme Being, is a passenger aboard every promise He makes because every trait in His character is either affirmed or denied by whether or not He keeps His promises. Every time a promise jet lands safely on the runway of fulfillment Father testifies that He is the mighty God He says He is. But were even a Piper Cub small, single-engine promise to crash before safely landing on that runway, everything that Father is would be on the fatality list. Simply put, having made promises, the only way Father can glorify Himself is by keeping them. Since glorifying Himself is what He's all about, you can be sure that He will keep His promises.[3]

2.

Assurance two that Father will keep His promises is *His track record of keeping them.* Teddy Roosevelt's riding with his men in Cuba. They come across American soldiers cowardly running from battle. Roosevelt pulls his gun, points it at the men, and says, 'Turn back and fight or I'll shoot you myself. If you don't believe I'll keep my word, just ask my men.' The craven men look at Roosevelt's Rough Riders. One of

---

3   Psalm 115:1; Romans 11:36.

the Riders says, 'He always does' while the others are all nodding their heads 'Yes!' Teddy's past keeping of his word was assurance he'd keep it now.[4]

The Bible nods its head with an enthusiastic 'Yes!' when you ask it if Father keeps His promises. Here are five examples from Father's promise-keeping track record.

Example one is *Father keeping His promise to give Abraham and Sarah a child.* Their biological clock made conception seem as far-fetched as Lazarus' coming from the tomb after his four-day hiatus in the cemetery. Yet we read, 'The Lord visited Sarah as he had said, and the Lord did to Sarah as he had promised. And Sarah conceived and bore Abraham a son in his old age at the time of which God had spoken to him.'[5] The message? Father *always* keeps His promises.

Example two is *Father keeping His promise to give Israel the land flowing with milk and honey.* In spite of the fear-producing unbelief of the ten spies and the Spartan fierce opposition of the inhabitants, Canaan became Jewish property. 'Thus the Lord gave to Israel all the land that he swore to give to their fathers. And they took possession of it, and they settled there…Not one word of all the good promises that the Lord had made to the house of Israel had failed; all came to pass.'[6] The message? Father *always* keeps His promises.

---

4   This story is factual. It's from one of the two volumes of William Bennett's *America: The Last Best Hope.* Unfortunately, I no longer have either of these volumes and am unable to give an accurate citation.

5   Genesis 21:1-2.

6   Joshua 21:43, 45.

Example three is *Father keeping His promise that the Messiah would be born in Bethlehem.* Through Micah the prophet Father promises that Bethlehem would be the Messiah's birthplace.[7] To keep this promise, He turns the heart of Caesar Augustus to take a census.[8] Registration for the census must be in one's hometown so Joseph has to travel from Nazareth to his Bethlehem birthplace. His pregnant wife Mary travels with him. Note now these words: 'And *while they were there*, the time came for her to give birth. And she gave birth to her firstborn son.'[9] Mind you, her water didn't break, her labor pains didn't begin, and her child wasn't born until she was *there*. Where? Bethlehem! The message? Father *always* keeps His promises.

Example four is *Father keeping His promise to Simeon that he wouldn't die until he had seen the Lord's Christ.* Like the good, good Father that He is, the Lord loves giving serendipity gifts to His children. He's promised His son Simeon that he won't die until he sees with his own eyes and touches with his own hands the Word made flesh. On *the very day* that Joseph and Mary bring their child Jesus to the temple to present Him to the Lord and at *the exact time* the presentation's taking place, Simeon comes into the temple. He takes Christ in his arms, and blesses the Father by saying, 'Lord, now you are letting your servant depart in peace, according to your word; for my eyes have seen your salvation.'[10] The message? Father *always* keeps His promises.

---

7 Micah 5:2.

8 Proverbs 21:1.

9 Proverbs 21:1; Luke 2:1-7, Emphasis added.

10 Luke 2:22-32.

Example five is *Father keeping His promise to Paul that he and all the crew of a ship they're on will survive the mother of all storms.* Luke describes the storm in the obituary words: 'When neither sun nor stars appeared for many days, and no small tempest lay on us, all hope of our being saved was at last abandoned.' They felt as hopeless as those stranded on the *Titanic* without lifeboats. But the Father who loves giving hope to His people in their hopeless situations sends Paul a coastguard rescue promise through an angel: 'Do not be afraid, Paul; you must stand before Caesar. And behold, God has granted you all those who sail with you.' A short time later all 276 people on the passenger manifesto feel sand between their toes as 'all were brought safely to land.'[11] The message? Father *always* keeps His promises.

The Father who kept these promises doesn't change.[12] What He was yesterday He is today. What He did yesterday He does today. He was the promise-keeping Father then. He is the promise-keeping Father now. His track record assures you He keeps His promises.

3.

Assurance three that Father keeps His promises is Jesus. Father's Grace Mona Lisa is the kept promise of the cross. The first brush stroke was in Eden's studio. 'I will put enmity between you and the woman and between your offspring and her offspring; he shall bruise your head and you shall bruise his heal.'[13] The canvas sat on the easel of history

---

11   Acts 27:21-44.
12   Malachi 3:6; James 1:17.
13   Genesis 3:15.

for centuries as Father added stroke after stroke from the pallet of His purpose. Finally, the time came to finish the salvation portrait. It could only be done with the red hues of judgment. Father doesn't hesitate. Jesus' cry, 'My God, my God why have you forsaken me?' is the Father keeping His first and hardest promise to humanity. Father's way of meeting our greatest need is by making and keeping His greatest promise.

Step into the gallery of amazing grace and pause and ponder the portrait of this kept promise. Behold the broken, battered, bleeding man hanging naked on that cross. What's going on? For the only time in human history a human being is experiencing hell on earth. Who is this person? The infinitely beloved Son of God. Why is this happening? Because the only way Father can keep Eden's promise is by subjecting His Son to Calvary's pains. Oh, if ever He's going to renege on a promise it will be now. But He doesn't. *He doesn't!* And the single conclusion to be drawn is that He will keep *every* promise He makes: 'He who did not spare his own Son but gave him up for us all, how will he not also with him graciously give us all things?'[14]

Child of the heavenly Father: you should be confident that He will keep every promise He makes you. Each is an infallible prediction. Each will be kept. Because of that you should be a promise-using Christian.

Let's look now at how you can become one.

---

14   Romans 8:32.

12

The Man Who Got Things From God

It would seem that our Lord finds our desires not too strong, but too weak. We are half-hearted creatures, fooling about with drink and sex and ambition when infinite joy is offered us, like an ignorant child who wants to go on making mud pies in a slum because he cannot imagine what is meant by the offer of a holiday at the sea. We are far too easily pleased.—C. S. Lewis[1]

George Mueller was known for engaging in a ministry to orphans that provided care for over ten thousand children in eighteenth-century England. He was called 'the man who got things from God' because he used his heavenly Father's promises to meet every need in the five orphanages he built.[2]

Your good, good Father wants *you* to be known as a man or woman who gets things from Him. He wants *you* to enjoy His goodness by tasting it in your own life again and again.

---

1   C. S. Lewis, *The Weight of Glory* (New York, NY: HarperCollins, 1980), 26.

2   One of the best biographies of Mueller is John Piper's character sketch entitled *George Mueller's Strategy for Showing God*. It can be found at desiringgod.org.

How do you do that? The same way Mueller did: by using your Father's promises. *Father wants you to use His promises to get good things from Him.*

The Old Testament believer named Jacob models the art of appropriating Father's goodness by using a promise in his dramatic high-noon showdown with his brother Esau. You're probably familiar with the story. With con-artist help from his mother Rebekah, Jacob steals Esau's blessing. The shock to Esau is equivalent to that of the only son of an older billionaire when he learns daddy's third and much younger wife has persuaded him to leave everything to her. Not surprisingly, Esau swears vengeance. Jacob's mother Rebekah sends him out of harm's way by relocating him with distant relatives.[3] There, Jacob marries twice, has twelve children, and, in spite of dealing with the spitting image of himself in his father-in-law Laban, becomes a successful businessman.[4] Years go by and then, suddenly, God orders Jacob to go home. The Lord cushions the difficult demand with a promise to do good to Jacob.[5] On the way home Jacob hears that Esau is heading toward him. Fearing that his brother's coming with the ill will with which Pharaoh pursued escaping Israel, Jacob claims the Lord's help by using His promise:

> And Jacob said, 'O God of my father Abraham and God of my father Isaac, O LORD who said to me, "Return to your country and to your kindred, that I may do you good," I am not worthy of the least of all the deeds of steadfast

---

3 Genesis 27.

4 Genesis 28-31.

5 Genesis 31:3, Genesis 32:12. Compare these with Genesis 28:15.

love and all the faithfulness that you have shown to your servant, for with only my staff I crossed this Jordan, and now I have become two camps. Please deliver me from the hand of my brother, from the hand of Esau, for I fear him, that he may come and attack me, the mothers with the children. **But you said, "I will surely do you good**, and make your offspring as the and of the sea, which cannot be numbered for multitude."[6]

Jacob models here the *six actions you must take to use a promise to enjoy a specific good from your Father.*

1.

The first action you must take to use a promise to enjoy the good it offers you is *that of finding a promise that speaks to your current situation.* Renowned nineteenth-century British General Charles G. Gordon models this promise-seeking habit. Next to his Bible, his most prized possession was Samuel Clarke's 'Precious Bible Promises.' The General would regularly search Clarke's for the promise best suited to his current need.[7] The question, *'What has God promised to do for me in this situation?'* dominated his living. It dominated Jacob's too. When he says to the Lord, 'But you said, "I will surely do you good"'[8] he's dining on a selected dish from Father's promise menu. You must do the same. Remember that just as there are shoes for every occasion—high-heels for weddings and cleats for football and jogging shoes for

---

6   Genesis 32:9-12. Emphasis added.

7   C. H. Spurgeon, *The Metropolitan Tabernacle Pulpit, Vol. 33* (Edinburgh: The Banner of Truth Trust, 1969), 4.

8   Genesis 32:12.

running and bedroom slippers for evenings at home—there are particular promises for every occasion. You must open the scriptural closet and select the right pair. You do this by asking, 'What has Father promised to do for me in this situation?'

Here are a couple of examples of this action. A preacher is preparing to preach. He asks, 'What has Father promised to do for me when I preach?' He recollects that Luke 11:13 promises him the Spirit's help and Isaiah 55:10-11 promises him the seed of the Word will produce Father's intended harvest. Or, say you've just sinned. A sense of guilt makes you feel nauseous. You ask, 'What anti-nausea promise has Father made that will help me now?' 1 John 1:9 tells you what He'll do for you in this situation. Over and over, again and again, as you go through your day you should be asking the 'What?' question: What has Father promised to do for me in this situation?

2.

The second action you must take to use a promise to enjoy the good it offers you is *that of fulfilling any condition attached to that promise.* If you wish to cash a check there are conditions you have to meet. You have to endorse the check and present identification proving you are the person to whom the check is written. Like checks, most promises have a condition you must meet to enjoy the good they offer. When Jacob says, 'O God of my father Abraham and God of my father, Isaac, O Lord who said to me, "Return to your country and to your kindred, that I may do you good"' he's declaring that by returning to his country he's meeting the condition for claiming the promise.[9] You must do the same with any condition attached to any promise you use if you wish to benefit from a promise.

Here are a couple of examples of this action. Your morale is crawling on its belly like a snail. Your 'What?' expedition has found a glorious promise: Father will make your spirit 'mount up with wings like eagles.' But there's a condition you must meet. It's as you 'wait on the Lord' that He'll put eagle fuel in your tank.[10] Again, here's a retired Christian who wants to use her time to serve the Lord as fully as a soldier serving her country. But she's not sure where the divine Commander wants to post her. She reports for duty with her 'What?' question and learns that Father will 'make straight (her) paths.' But there's a double condition she must meet. It's as she 'trust(s) in the Lord with all (her) heart' and refuses to 'lean on (her) own understanding'[11] that her orders will come.

If you wish to enjoy a sacred sweet you must fulfill any condition attached to the promise offering it to you.

3.

The third action you must take to use a promise to enjoy the good it offers you is *that of bringing the promise to Father in prayer*. When Jacob says, 'O God of my father Abraham …' he's praying.[12] Praying a promise is equivalent to *presenting* a check to the bank for cashing. After you've found a suitable

---

9   Genesis 32:9.

10   Isaiah 40:30-31.

11   Proverbs 3:5-6.

12   Genesis 32:9.

promise and met its condition, you're to present it for cashing by asking Father to keep it and give you the blessing it offers. Remember the Lord Jesus' words: 'If you then, who are evil, know how to give good gifts to your children, how much more will your Father who is in heaven give good things *to those who ask him!*'[13]

4.

The fourth action you must take to use a promise to enjoy the good it offers you is *that of expecting Father to keep the promise.* Two soldiers are close friends as well as brothers in arms. One of them is injured and stranded. The other is ordered to make no attempt to rescue him. He disobeys and goes after his buddy. He comes back to camp carrying his dead friend and bleeding from serious wounds. His commander says, 'This is why I didn't want you to go. Now I've lost both of you!' The injured rescuer says, 'Sir, it was worth it. When I got to him he said, "Jim, I knew you'd come."'[14]

You should present a promise to Father with a similar 'I know you'll keep it' expectancy. Jacob does. Notice that after praying 'he stays there that night.'[15] He makes no attempt to escape. Why not? Because he expects Father to keep His promise. When you present a promise to Father you ought to be the way you are when you order a book from Amazon. You expect it to be delivered. You look for it in the

---

13   Matthew 7:11.

14   John Maxwell, *Winning with People* (Nashville, TN: Thomas Nelsen, Inc., 2004), 170.

15   Genesis 32:13.

mail. Except sometimes Amazon packages get lost. Father's promises never do. He delivers every one of them.

5.

The fifth action that you must take to use a promise to enjoy the good it offers you is *that of acknowledging Father's goodness in giving you the promised sacred sweet.* When I was a boy my mother ingrained in me the importance of thanking people who'd been kind to me. Whenever I received a gift or a compliment she'd say, 'Now, Charley, what do you say?' Jacob demonstrates what you're to say to your heavenly Father when He keeps a promise and gives you its good. The end of this chapter of his life finds him coming safely to the city of Shechem. 'There he erected an altar and called it El-Elohe-Israel.'[16] The title means 'God, the God of Israel.' Jacob's doing what Noah did after leaving the ark and Zechariah did after his son John was born and Simeon did after he saw the infant Jesus.[17] Like them, he's praising Father for keeping His promise. Kept promises are dry-seasoned wood for the fire of praise. The moment you experience one you ought to say, 'Bless the Lord, O my soul, and all that is within me, bless his holy name! Bless the Lord, O my soul, and forget not all his benefits.'[18] This pleases and delights Father. It's His way of glorifying Himself in your life. He gives you grace (by keeping His promises) so you'll give Him glory (by praising and thanking Him for keeping them).

---

16 Genesis 33:20.

17 Genesis 8:20-21; Luke 1:67-79; Luke 2:25-32.

18 Psalm 103:1-2.

6.

The sixth action you must take to use a promise to enjoy the good it offers you is that of making promise-using your habit. Arthur said of his knights, 'I make them place their hands in mine and swear allegiance to the king.' Jacob calling God 'El-Elohe-Israel' is not only his expression of gratitude; it's also his swearing allegiance to Father. He's saying, 'Lord, I will be yours.' Allegiance to Father involves living by faith. And living by faith is living by using promises to enjoy Father's help again and again. In essence, then, Jacob is committing to living this way.

Father wants you to do the same. He wants you to do this because He's determined to get glory from you by being good to you and one of the primary ways He does you good is by keeping promises as you claim them.

7.

Begin taking these six actions to use Father's promises and you'll soon become a Christian who gets the good things they offer you.

I pray all that you've read thus far is encouraging you to begin using Father's promises every day, all day long. Father wants that for you. We'll see why in the next chapter.

13
S.D.G.

*It is a cause of much weakness to many that they do not treat the
promises of God as realities. If a friend makes them a promise,
they regard it as a substantial thing, and look for that which
it secures; but the declarations of God are often viewed as so
many words which mean very little. This is most dishonoring to
the Lord, and very injurious to ourselves.*—C. H. Spurgeon[1]

Johann Sebastian Bach often wrote the letters *SDG* at the
end of a musical composition. They stand for *Sola Deo
Gloria*: to God alone be glory.[2] Father wants you to begin
using His promises so you can begin writing these letters on
the pages of your everyday living. Abraham exemplifies this:

> In hope he believed against hope, that he should become
> the father of many nations, as he had been told, 'So shall
> your offspring be.' He did not weaken in faith when he

---

1   Charles H. Spurgeon, *According to Promise or The Lord's Method
     of Dealing with His Chosen People* (Ichthus Publications edition,
     2014), 36-37.

2   https://www.christianity.com/church/church-history/church-
     history-for-kids/j-s-bach-soli-deo-gloria-to-the-glory-of-god-
     alone-11635057.html See also Jane Stuart Smith and Betty Carlson,
     The Gift of Music (Wheaton, IL: Crossway Books, 1987), 38.

considered his own body, which was as good as dead (since he was about a hundred years old), or when he considered the barrenness of Sarah's womb. No unbelief made him waver concerning the promise of God, but he grew strong in his faith as he gave glory to God, fully convinced that God was able to do what he had promised.[3]

The message of Abraham's example is: *you glorify God by optimistically using His promises to enjoy His Fatherly goodness.*

1.

These words reiterate the truth Father wants you to focus on: He wants you to use His promises optimistically. He wants you to imitate Abraham. You imitate him by being 'strong in faith'[4] And that means being *optimistic.* Optimistic about the Father's intention to keep His promises!

That's really what faith is you know. It's being 'fully persuaded'[5]—optimistic!—about God's promise-keeping. Find faith in action anywhere—whether in a patriarch facing a parent's worst nightmare,[6] or in a prostitute experiencing mercy before an invading army,[7] or in a prophet preparing for disaster,[8] and you'll find that faith is optimism in action. If you want to know what it means to believe it means being optimistic about your Father.

---

3   Romans 4:18-21.

4   Romans 4:20.

5   Romans 4:20-21.

6   Hebrews 11:17-19 and Genesis 22:5.

7   Hebrews 11:31 and Joshua 6:22-23.

8   Habakkuk 2:4 and 3:17-19.

This optimism that's faith is optimism *about Father's grace coming through a 'promise'*[9] from Him. The Christian life is a life of faith from start to finish because it's a life of optimism about Father's promises from start to finish. Your Christian life *began* with optimism that Father would keep His promise to drop all His charges against you, take you off death row, release you from prison, and accept you as totally as He accepts Jesus—all because of Jesus' righteousness.[10] Your faith *continues* as your optimism about Father daily draws from His grace by depending on His promises as a little child depends on its parents for everything from food to clothing to shelter to protection.[11]

The optimism that's faith depends on Father's promises by *focusing expectantly* on them. *Expectantly,* by being 'fully convinced' that God 'is able to do what he' promises[12] no matter the obstacles. *Focusing,* by preoccupying yourself with His promises as a vain woman with her looks, a politician with re-election, and a vegan with his diet.

As you use Father's promises by claiming them optimistically you'll begin *enjoying the good they offer you every day, all day long.* Daily claiming His promises the way a thirsty man uses water to quench His thirst you'll find Father giving you the good things He promises just as He did with Abraham.[13]

---

9   Romans 4:20.

10 Romans 4:22; Acts 16:31; Galatians 2:16.

11 2 Corinthians 5:7; Galatians 2:20; Colossians 2:6-7.

12 Romans 4:21.

13 The outcome of Abraham's faith as described in Romans 4:18-21 was the birth of Isaac, Genesis 21:1-2.

Abraham exemplifies the lifestyle of optimistically using Father's promises that Father wants you to live.

2.

Father wants you to use His promises optimistically because *using them this way gives Him* 'glory.'[14] It's not the *only* way you glorify Him. But *it is* the *primary* way you do that just as it was for Abraham. Love *isn't* the only ingredient in the recipe for a great marriage; but it *is* the primary one. Expecting Father to keep His promises is to His glory what love is to a good marriage because the root of glorifying Him in any way, shape, or form ultimately boils down to expecting Him to be true to His word. Faith honors Him; unbelief dishonors Him. And the core of faith is optimism that Father will do what He promises.[15]

3.

The reason expecting Father to keep His word glorifies Him is that this expectation *treats Him as the peerless person He is.* He declares that He's one of a kind: 'I am the first and I am the last; besides me there is no god.'[16] This isn't an idle boast. It's a fact. The longest running show in history isn't on Broadway. It's on the stage of the Father's display of His greatness. There He shows His encore excellence, eliciting curtain call after curtain call to standing-ovation praise. And one of His best roles is that of promise maker and promise keeper. When He keeps promises that seem impossible to

---

14   Romans 4:20.

15   Habakkuk 2:4; Hebrews 11:6

16   Isaiah 44:6.

keep, He acts as only He can. He acts like God. So, when you're optimistic that He'll keep His promises to you, you exalt Him by saying, 'Who is like you, O Lord, among the gods? Who is like you, majestic in holiness, awesome in glorious deeds, doing wonders?'[17] This glorifies Him.

4.

Your expectation that Father will keep His promises doesn't just honor Him with a vague recognition that He's peerless. *It is, in fact, a prism refracting the light of Father's specific glory into its rainbow beauty.* Here are a handful of the ways this expectation does this.

A.

When you optimistically use Father's promises to enjoy the good they offer you, you glorify Him by *glorifying His ability.* The late baseball pitcher Dizzy Dean loved to blow his own horn. A woman once scolded him for bragging. 'Ma'am,' Dizzy said, 'it ain't braggin' when you can do it. And I can do it!' When you expect Father to keep a promise, especially one as humanly impossible to keep as the promise to give ancient Abraham and Sarah a child, you're declaring your optimism that Father can do it. You're affirming that He's 'able to do what he had promised.'[18] You're answering the question, 'Is anything too hard for the Lord'[19] with a resounding, 'For nothing will be impossible with God.'[20] This glorifies Him.

---

17   Exodus 15:11.

18   Romans 4:21.

19   Genesis 18:14.

20   Luke 1:37.

B.

When you optimistically use Father's promises to enjoy the good they offer you, you glorify Him by *declaring He's trustworthy.* You aren't saying what the leper says to Jesus: 'Lord, if you are willing, you can make me clean.'[21] There's no need. You're affirming that the very fact that Father has made a promise expresses His willingness to keep it. By claiming a promise you're saying, 'Lord, I'm optimistic that you mean what you say.' This glorifies Him.

C.

When you optimistically use Father's promises to enjoy the good they offer you, you glorify Him by *glorifying Jesus.* The late Anglican John Stott shares a story that makes the point. When Scottish missionary Frederick Arnot was a teen he and friends would stand outside Glasgow taverns and preach the gospel. They'd sing a hymn to draw a crowd then talk about Jesus. One Saturday they drew a particularly sodden group of men. They listened to the music but when it stopped and the preaching started they mocked the junior missionaries. The pattern goes on for a while until finally the boys are ready to surrender. As Arnot's leaving he feels a hand on his shoulder. He turns and looks into the face of a tall Scot. The man says, 'Keep at it, laddie. God loves to hear men speak well of His Son.'[22]

Using Father's promises speaks well of His Son because it acknowledges that every good Father promises you is a specific

---

21 Luke 5:12, NIV.

22 This is from an Urbana Compendium I no longer have in my library. The anecdote illustrates the thrust of John 8:54 and Philippians 2:9-11.

good that He's secured for you and gives to you through Jesus.[23] Simply put, when you claim a promise through Jesus you declare Jesus' greatness. This glorifies Father.[24]

D.

When you optimistically use Father's promises to enjoy the good they offer you, you glorify Him by *enjoying Him.* Genesis 21 tells us that the result of Abraham's optimistic use of Father's promise was the good of Isaac's birth: 'The Lord visited Sarah as he had said, and the Lord did to Sarah as he promised. And Sarah conceived and bore Abraham a son in his old age at the time of which God had spoken to him.'[25] Abraham tasted and saw the goodness of the Lord. Meaning, he enjoyed having God as his God.[26] No doubt he thanked God more profusely than the returning leper thanked Jesus.

Every time Father keeps a promise and gives you the good it offers you, He's giving you reason to imitate the Psalmist: 'I will praise the name of God with a song; I will magnify him with thanksgiving' (Ps. 69:30). Thanking Him acknowledges Him as the giver of the good you enjoy. This glorifies Father.

E.

When you optimistically use Father's promises to enjoy the good they offer you, you glorify Him *by living the way Jesus lived.* Our Lord was the quintessential promise user.

---

23   2 Corinthians 1:20.

24   Ephesians 2:9-11.

25   Genesis 21:1-2.

26   Genesis 12:3.

He lived by faith.[27] He lived with absolute optimism that Father would keep the promises He made to Him as the Redeemer.[28] You see this in the fact that Psalm 22 was on Jesus' mind when He was on the cross. This Psalm speaks of a man who is more than conqueror over indescribable heartache by being optimistic that God will deliver him. It cameos Christ. Our Lord managed the agony of the cross through the ecstasy of His Father's promise of 'joy set before him.'[29] Thus, when you live by Father's promises you live like Jesus. This is Father's desire and design for you.[30] It's what Jesus means when He tells you to 'follow me.'[31] Optimistically using Father's promises, then, means living the way Father wants. This glorifies Him.

5.

Father makes clear through Abraham's example that He weds His glory to our using His promises optimistically. What He has joined together we dare not put asunder. It's not an exaggeration to say that you can no more glorify Father as He wants without using His promises optimistically, than you can grow cotton without planting seed or lose weight properly without eating healthily or maintain a budget without disciplined spending. This is because He gets glory from you by giving grace to you, and one of the primary ways

---

27   Hebrews 12:2.

28   Psalm 2:7-9; Psalm 22.

29   Hebrews 12:2.

30   Romans 8:29; 2 Corinthians 3:18.

31   Matthew 9:9.

He gives grace to you is through your using His promises with optimism that He'll keep them.

Here's the truth of the matter: Father is determined to get glory from you by giving grace to you by keeping His promises to do you good.

There's only one response you can give such grace.

SDG.

6.

When you immediately begin emphasizing Father's promises in your every day living by seeing them as *His M.O.* for doing good to you, you take **Step Two** toward becoming acquainted with Him as the Father who delights in being good to you through His promises.

Take this step now.

After all, if Father makes a big deal of His promises shouldn't you?

7.

Now that you've begun making much of having God as your Father and making much of His promises as His M.O. for doing you good you're ready to begin using His promises to enjoy the good they offer you. **Step Three** will help you begin doing this by giving you a handful of promises you can begin using immediately to enjoy your Father's goodness NOW.

Let's look at these promises.

3

Step Three to Knowing God as He Wants to Be Known:

You must immediately begin using His promises to experience Fatherly good now.

14
Straw

Father has spread over the Bible 'a perfect wealth of promises, suitable to every kind of experience and every condition of life...Their name is legion...There are 'shalls' and 'wills' in God's treasury for every condition. About God's infinite mercy and compassion—about His readiness to receive all who repent and believe—about His willingness to forgive, pardon, and absolve the chief of sinners—about His power to change hearts and alter our corrupt nature—about the encouragement to pray, and hear the gospel, and draw near to the throne of grace—about strength for duty, comfort in trouble, guidance in perplexity, help in sickness, consolation in death, support under bereavement, happiness beyond the grave, reward in glory—about all these things there is an abundant supply of promises in the Word. No one can form an idea of its abundance unless he carefully searches the Scriptures, keeping the subject steadily in view. If any one doubts it, I can only say, "Come and see."—J. C. Ryle[1]

This isn't a Pharaoh book. Remember the Egyptian villain as he's pictured on the post office wall in Exodus? His crime

1   John Piper, *Future Grace* (Sisters, OR: Multnomah Books, 1995), 15-16.

was demanding bricks without giving straw.[2] He told Israel what to do without helping them do it.

This book emphasizes that Father is determined to get glory from you by being good to you. It stresses that a primary way He's good to you is through His promises. It insists that He wants you to use His promises to enjoy this good. So you need the straw of some promises to get you started making the bricks of enjoying His Fatherly goodness *now*.

Thankfully, there's no shortage of straw. The Bible's a bale-filled field of promissory straw. Estimates place the number of God's promises between 3,000 and 7,000. This means I must be as choosy in the first promises I recommend as Duke University basketball's Coach K is in deciding whom to give a basketball scholarship.

How do you decide which promises to recommend to begin enjoying good gifts when you've got such a cornucopia of choices? In the same way you decide which doctor or dentist or movie or book to recommend to someone: by personal experience. For example, if you asked me, 'Charley, could you recommend a good book on the Christian attitude toward life?' I'd say without hesitation, 'Sure—I recommend *Grace-Focused Optimism* by C. L. Chase!' Saw that coming, huh? Sorry. I couldn't resist.

But you get the point. By definition, a recommendation is as personalized as your DNA. We recommend what *we've* found good or helpful or beneficial. Because of this, the promises that make up this section are promises that *I, by grace, have used* to 'taste and see that the Lord is good.'

---

2   Exodus 5:6-9.

The '80s American Express commercial told me about their credit card, 'Don't leave home without it.' I never leave home without these promises in my mental wallet. And I can tell you from experience that they work. Father keeps them. By grace I've enjoyed the good they offer to His glory and my good.

Each of the promises in the following bale deals with some good the *Father offers to do us NOW amid the stresses and struggles of following Jesus in our everyday living.* Each shows us a particular help Father will give us to get glory from us by assisting us in living the abundant life He sent Jesus to give us.

There are eight of these promises. We'll look at each following the format of *content, condition,* and *claiming.* First, we'll consider the specific good a particular promise contains. Second, we'll consider the promise's condition: what does it ask you to do in order to enjoy its goodness? Third, we'll think about when to claim the promise by suggesting the appropriate time to use it.

Let's gather some straw.

15
The G.O.O.D. Life

It is a rule, in interpreting the Word of God, that the promises made to the natural Israel, so far as they are spiritual, belong to the spiritual Israel. Believers in Christ are the true seed of Abraham... The covenant made with Abraham is a covenant made with all who are in Abraham, with all the seed born according to promise, as was Isaac; and we may lay hold, without doubt or hesitancy, upon all the spiritual promises made to the seed of Israel...I have, therefore, no doubt whatever in taking such a promise as this, and using it with reference to the whole company of God's elect—those peculiar people, whom God has created for himself, who shall show forth his praise.—Charles H. Spurgeon, commenting on God's promise in Jeremiah 32:41.[1]

Father wants you to go through every day with the optimism that He has a day full of good He's ready to do you. This optimism, itself a good God promises to give you, is as indispensable to your enjoying other promises as light is to seeing. But staying optimistic is as difficult as walking safely through a minefield. Not because Father isn't worthy of our

---

1   C. H. Spurgeon, *The Metropolitan Tabernacle Pulpit, Volume 34* (Edinburgh: The Banner of Truth Trust, 1970), 422.

optimism. He is—eminently so—but because our optimism is easily crippled by shrapnel from our moods, meanderings, and miseries. So, Father gives us a high-octane optimism-fueling promise to help us stay as optimistic about Him as newlyweds are about their future as they walk out of church into life. It's found in Jeremiah 32:40-41:

> I will make with them an everlasting covenant, that I will not turn away from doing good to them. And I will put the fear of me in their hearts, that they may not turn from me. I will rejoice in doing them good, and I will plant them in this land in faithfulness, with all my heart and all my soul.

Here Father promises you that your life is Grace G.O.O.D.

1.

The *content* of this promise is *optimism that flows from understanding what it means for you to be a Christian*. Being a Christian means your life is a Grace G.O.O.D. The acronym stands for a **G**od (as Father) **O**rchestrated **O**ccasion for **D**emonstration of Father's determination to get glory from you by being good to you.

The '**G**' in the acronym stands for *God*. Notice how this promise gives top billing to what He will do for you: His 'I will' occurs five times in these two verses. Behind this is the emphatic biblical insistence that the Lord is *always* the One dealing with us.[2] How does He deal with us *all the time*? Not as our Creator, King, and Judge but as our *Father*. His Fatherhood is the central nervous system of His entire relationship with us. It's the gated spiritual community in

---

2   Genesis 50:20; Romans 11:36; Ephesians 1:11.

which we live. It governs all His dealings with us. He is always being Father with and to us.

The first '**O**' stands for *orchestration*. Father's 'I wills' in this promise are not written in erasable pencil. They're written in the indelible ink of certainty. He will do for us what He promises. How can He make such a bold boast and give us such an awesome assurance? Because He orchestrates our lives. He writes every note on our life's staff from our earthly conception to our earthly conclusion. You can say to everything at every moment of every day what Jesus says to Pilate, 'You would have no authority over me at all unless it had been given you from above.'[3] Whatever is in your life now is there because Father sees fit for it to be there.

The second '**O**' stands for *occasion*. An occasion is a time of focusing on something specific. Birthdays, anniversaries, and retirement parties are occasions because they focus on the specifics of birth, marriage, and the cessation of a lifetime of work. Our lives as believers are occasions for Father to do something specific for us. They are the venue for Him to 'make' and 'do' and 'plant' for us. This means your life isn't a stray balloon somersaulting wildly in the wind of chance or even, ultimately, your choices or others' choices. Father's brought you into existence for a specific purpose.

The '**D**' stands for *demonstration*.[4] It tells you the glorious truth that Father has brought you into existence for the specific purpose of demonstrating *His goodness* to you.

Notice three ways He stresses this in this promise:

---

3   John 19:11.

4   Jay Adams, *The Grand Demonstration* (Santa Barbara, CA: EastGate Publishers, 1991).

Father stresses that He's brought you into existence for the specific purpose of being good to you by *promising you that doing you good IS His purpose in your life.* He says, 'I will do them good.' Remember, as a believer you're on the passenger list of the pronoun 'them.' Father's talking about you. He's talking about His plan for you. I say with reverence, He's got a one-track mind when it comes to you. The only thing on His 'to-do' list under your name is 'Be good to him / her.'

Father stresses that He's brought you into existence for the specific purpose of being good to you by *promising you that He'll CONTINUOUSLY do you good.* He says, 'I will not turn away from doing good to them.' None of the things that make us turn from doing good affect Him. *Fatigue* won't make His muscles ache so deeply He longs for a break. *Distraction's* heavy snow won't make Him ground the planes of His goodness. The fact He has His eye on everything else doesn't mean He ever takes His eye off of you. The *shameful failure to show appreciation* won't put a stop order on the checks of His goodness. Even your *failures* won't make Him suspend His goodness like a parent confiscating a tenth grader's cell phone for bad grades. When you've eaten forbidden fruit He'll come walking in your garden in the cool of the day to show you the goodness of His mercy. His goodness carries no expiration date. 'The steadfast love of the Lord never ceases; his mercies never come to an end; they are new every morning; great is your faithfulness.'[5]

Father stresses that He's brought you into existence for the specific purpose of being good to you by *promising you that He gets enormous PLEASURE from being good to you.*

---

5   Lamentations 3:22-23.

Modern psychology speaks of 'flow.' Flow is the sheer elation you feel when you're doing what you love doing. Father tells us in this promise that He experiences divine flow by being good to us: 'I will rejoice in doing them good…with all my heart and with all my soul.' Father isn't as reluctant to do you good as a man giving his Rolex to an armed robber. He doesn't do you good begrudgingly like a presidential candidate conceding a close election he expected to win. And He doesn't do you good half-heartedly, throwing in the change in His pocket the way you do with the Salvation Army kettle at Christmas. He does you good as wholeheartedly— as generously, gladly, and enthusiastically—as a mother gives herself to her newborn. Why? Because He loves being good to you. It brings Him joy! Nothing gives Father greater pleasure than being good to His children.

What shall we say to these things? Don't they make you want to sing the doxology and devote yourself to loving and living for such a good, good Father? And doesn't this promise give you invincible reason to be optimistic about *all* of Father's promises to do you good?

2.

The *condition* for experiencing the good this promise offers you is *personalizing* it. The famous Scottish theology professor and preacher 'Rabbi' John Duncan once told a woman who was hesitant to come to the Lord's table, 'Take it, woman, it's for sinners!' Father says to you about this promise, 'Take it, child, it's for you!' One way you can do that is by making 'Your life is a Grace G.O.O.D.' into the personal '*My* life is a Grace G.O.O.D.' You can do that because this promise is as much yours as your fingerprints. Your core and governing view of yourself is to be 'My life is a Grace G.O.O.D.'

3.

One helpful way of *claiming* this promise is by turning it into a prayer by saying, 'Father, thank you that my life is a Grace G.O.O.D.' Do this as you *start your day.* Pour yourself a cup of this grace coffee as you wake by saying, 'Father, thank you that I wake to a Grace G.O.O.D. day.' *Continue this as you go through your day.* Face your day's interruptions, disruptions, and eruptions by saying of each, 'Father, thank you that *this* is a Grace G.O.O.D.' *Likewise*, as crises, challenges, and calamities pelt you like large hailstones in a bad storm say of each, 'Father, thank you that *even this* is a Grace G.O.O.D.'

Since staying optimistic about Father and His promises is crucial to enjoying good gifts it's good to find *a practical way* to stay focused on this Grace G.O.O.D. promise. If you use a prayer book to begin your day (as I sometimes do), you might want to write that sentence across the first page. Or you might order an inexpensive rubber bracelet with the letters G.O.O.D on it and wear it on your wrist as a constant reminder. Or you might want to write it at the top of your to-do list or your daily planner/calendar. But whether you follow these suggestions, or choose another method, having a physical/tangible way of focusing on this promise as you begin your day, go through your day, and when trouble knocks, will help you live as the optimist about His promises Father wants you to be. And this will help you enjoy the good of Father's other promises by enabling you to be optimistic about them.

4.

Everyone wants to live the good life. Father tells you that you *are* living the good life. You're living the good life because your life is a Grace G.O.O.D. Your life from start to finish, every day, all day long is *a God (as Father) orchestrated occasion for the demonstration of His goodness to you.*

You can say of yourself, 'My life is a Grace G.O.O.D.'

You can look at whatever happens to you and say, 'Thank You, Father, that this is a Grace G.O.O.D.'

Don't you think that gives you reason to be optimistic about all of Father's promises every day, all day long?

16
What Oscar Wilde Couldn't Do But You Can!

Q8: What is meant by deliverance from evil? A. That if God sees meet to permit us to be tempted by Satan, and the wicked without, or by our own hearts within, to sin; or occasionally, by his providence; that he will not leave us, but undertake for us, that we may not be led into sin thereby, but by his grace be made more than conquerors…According to his promise; 1 Corinthians 10:13, But God is faithful, who will not suffer you to be tempted above that ye are able.—John Flavel[1]

Temptation.

Solicitation to sin pulling on you like gravity on a suicidal man who's just leaped from the fortieth floor of a Manhattan skyscraper. A commercial from Satan soliciting you with the 'fleeting pleasures of sin'[2] that's so slick it makes the best car salesman in the world seem tongue-tied and inept. And, if you're like me, something you wake up to every morning as a soldier in a foxhole wakes to another day of battle.

---

1   John Flavel, *The Works of John Flavel, Vol. VI* (Edinburgh: The Banner of Truth Trust, 1968 reprint), 314.

2   Hebrews 11:25.

Oscar Wilde famously said, 'I can resist anything but temptation.' You may feel that way too. Especially with that Delilah sin that often cuts your hair and leaves you as weak as Samson grinding in the Philistine-mill of shame and failure.[3]

Take heart. 1 Corinthians 10:13 places in your hands a sharp two-edged sword promise you can use to conquer even a temptation that seems as irresistible as Eve found the forbidden fruit: 'No temptation has overtaken you that is not common to man. God is faithful, and he will not let you be tempted beyond your ability, but with the temptation he will also provide the way of escape, that you may be able to endure it.' *Father promises you He'll help you beat the devil when he throws his best at you.*

1.

The *content* of this promise is the Lord's assurance that *He'll help you defeat any temptation the devil presents you.* Johnny Unitas is one of the greatest quarterback's in N.F.L. history. He played for the Baltimore Colts. Teammate Tom Matte said that because of Unitas the Colts knew they could beat any team they faced. Father tells you in this promise that because of Him you can resist any temptation you face as surely and heroically as Joseph said 'No!' to Mrs. Potiphar.[4]

Like the manager of a boxer who never lets his man get into the ring with a fighter bigger and better than he is, Father 'will not let you be tempted beyond your ability.' Like a mother watching her three-year-old playing in the shallow

---

3   Judges Chapter 16.

4   Genesis 39:9-12.

water of the Gulf of Mexico, ready to move to his rescue in the blink of an eye were something to happen, Father will 'provide the way of escape' for every temptation you face. This means that you can 'endure' any temptation in the sense of knocking it out instead of allowing it to knock you out.

With Father's help you can beat the devil when he throws his best at you.

2.

Like many other promises, the *condition* for claiming this one is *believing* Father. But tender wounds from past failures may make you find it as hard to believe this as Sarah found believing that she was going to be a ninety-year-old mother. You might even be tempted to scoff like your ancient cousin.[5] 'After all,' you say in your defense as you talk about your defeats by a specific temptation, 'I've got lots of bloody noses and black eyes from times in the ring with it.' Still, this promise gives you a compelling reason not to throw in the towel and concede the fight. That reason is Father is 'faithful.' His faithfulness is His you-can-take-it-to-the bank utter reliability. If He tells you His help is enough you can be sure it is. Like the rest of His promissory checks, this one won't bounce. Believe it and you'll see.

With Father's help you can beat the devil when he throws his best at you.

3.

There are two times when it's best to *claim* this promise.

---

5   Genesis 18:9-15.

A.

First, you should claim it *proactively.* If you're about to go on an Atlantic cruise and you're prone to seasickness you are proactive by bringing along motion sickness pills. If you're going to the beach and you're prone to burn, you are proactive by bringing along high-powered sunscreen. If you're going into flu season and you're high risk because of your age you are proactive by getting vaccinated.

Similarly, you have known areas of temptation that are as dangerous to you as a poison ivy bush to someone allergic to that weed. Knowing this, use this promise proactively. Claim it *before* you go into a danger zone. Here are some examples:

Example one of using 1 Corinthians 10:13 proactively: You're a high school basketball coach. A disgruntled parent has asked to meet with you to talk about his daughter's lack of playing time. You know you'll be tempted to say something you'll regret. Claim this promise before the meeting.

Example two of using 1 Corinthians 10:13 proactively: You're a mom who wakes every day to the ups and downs of caring for a two-year-old and a four-year-old. You know before you get out of bed that the coming day will test your patience, siphon your energy, and make you question whether being a mother's quite the blessing it's supposed to be. Claim this promise before you start your day.

Example three of using 1 Corinthians 10:13 proactively: Like Abraham with his Sarah or Naomi with her Elimelech[6] you're facing the death of your spouse. You know this will be a time of great sadness and challenging adjustment.

---

6   Genesis 23; Ruth 1:2-3.

Your heart's desire is to honor the Lord by not grieving as unbelievers 'who have no hope'[7] and by honoring the One whose 'power is made perfect in weakness.'[8] Claim this promise as the time approaches.

B.

The second time to claim this promise is *reactively.* You know from experience that temptation often ambushes you. Someone speaks a harsh word to you by blaming you for something you didn't do or by putting you down in front of others and you're tempted to fight fire with fire; an attractive person walks by and lust begs you to look lasciviously; rain cancels an outdoor concert you're looking forward to and the temptation to grumble rises like a rioting crowd. Right then and there, claim 1 Corinthians 10:13 as a shield by calling on Father to help you resist.

Do this and you'll find again and again: with Father's help you can beat the devil when he throws his best at you.

With Father's help you can do what Oscar Wilde couldn't do.

---

7   1 Thessalonians 4:13.

8   2 Corinthians 12:9.

17

The Highway to the Land of Beginning Again

When the meal was over, Jesus turned to Peter and said—what?—'How could you have denied me?'—'Do you still think yourself worthy to be with the disciples?'—'What is the difference between your sin and the sin of Judas?' No, not that, not a single reference to the past, or the dark tragedy of Peter's denial; but this: 'Lovest thou me?' When Peter had been given an opportunity to confess his love three times, as he had thrice denied Jesus, then Jesus said to him, 'Feed my sheep.' The past was blotted out; its dark sin was forgiven and forgotten. Peter is restored to his place as an Apostle, and is given another chance...Christianity is a highway that leads to the Land of Beginning Again.—Clarence Edward Macartney[1]

The illustrious Alexander Whyte is preaching in Edinburgh. He leans over the pulpit and tells the congregation he's about to identify the biggest sinner in the city. Suddenly the sanctuary's as silent as a broken radio. Everyone's as tense and attentive as a Parris Island marine before his Drill Sgt.

---

1   Clarence Edward Macartney, *Peter and His Lord* (Nashville, TN: Cokesbury Press, 1938), 117, 119.

Whyte says, 'The name of the greatest sinner in Edinburgh is — Alexander Whyte!'[2]

I routinely feel like the greatest sinner in my town. And my house. And around my friends. Don't you? Because, let's face it, in spite of Father's available help we sometimes say 'Yes' to temptation. We fail the way Abraham, Sarah, David, Jonah, and Peter did.[3] We sin.

Praise God, He makes a gracious good available to us even when we fail Him. His grace is the land of beginning again. And the highway to it is the promise He makes us in 1 John 1:9: 'If we confess our sins, he is faithful and just to forgive us our sins and to cleanse us from all unrighteousness.' *Father promises to forgive every sin you confess.*

1.

The *content* of this promise is Father's assurance He'll do you the good of *forgiving you*. When He forgives you He treats you the way the prodigal's father treated him when he returned from the far country. He says, 'Bring quickly the best robe, and put it on him, and put a ring on his hand, and shoes on his feet. And bring the fattened calf and kill it, and let us eat and celebrate. For this my son was dead, and is alive again; he was lost, and is found.'[4] Father forgiving you is Father welcoming you back to fellowship with open arms and the generous pledge He'll even help you deal with any consequences of your sin.

---

2   G. F. Barbour, *The Life of Alexander Whyte* (London: Hodder and Stoughton Limited, 1923), 316.

3   Genesis 12:10-20; Genesis 16:1-6; 2 Samuel 11; Jonah 1; Luke 22:54-62.

4   Luke 15:22-24.

2.

The *condition* for enjoying this promised good is *confession of sin*. Psalm 51 models true confession. It shows that we confess when we turn to Father and *incriminate ourselves* as honestly as a dying criminal admitting his crimes.[5] It teaches us that confession is *verbalizing* to Him that we've failed Him miserably.[6] It reminds us that confession involves *grieving* over our sin because it's a deeply personal offense against Father Himself[7] and is indescribably wrong.[8] It shows that confession involves *blaming no one but ourselves* for the sin.[9] Yet, in spite of our sin's foulness, it stresses that we're to confess with *optimism* that Father will forgive us when we confess because He will![10]

As a Christian you know that the Psalm points to the cleansing that comes from the blood of Jesus.[11] So, it's through Jesus that you ask Father to forgive you. And it's through Jesus that you confess with optimism because through 'the blood of Jesus his Son' Father 'cleanses from *all* sin.'[12]

---

5   For a helpful exposition of Psalm 51 see Robert Candlish, *The Prayer of a Broken Heart* (Birmingham, AL: Solid Ground Christian Books, ND).

6   Psalm 51:1-3.

7   Psalm 51:4.

8   Psalm 51:4.

9   Note the personal pronoun 'I' and 'My' throughout the Psalm.

10   Psalm 51:17.

11   1 John 1:7; 1 John 2:1-2.

12   1 John 1:7. Emphasis added.

3.

The *time to claim this promise* is when you sin. You should claim it *any time and every time you sin*. You should claim it *immediately*, the moment you're aware you've sinned, confessing and asking for forgiveness as quickly as Peter asked Jesus to help him when sinking in the sea.[13] And, again, you should claim it *repeatedly* because Father will forgive you through Jesus again and again as He did Abraham, David, Jonah, Peter, and the sinful woman in the Pharisee's house.[14] Father promises He'll forgive you the moment you confess.

4.

What about your *bully* sin? That's the sin that seizes you by the throat with a windpipe-crushing, asphyxiating sense of guilt. You gasp for breath as Satan and your heart gang up on you to make you feel as hopeless as Judas. You cower in shame. You question whether you're really a Christian. You join Adam and Eve in thinking you need to hide from the Lord. You echo Paul's kidney-stone lament 'Wretched man that I am!'[15] And you wonder if you can begin again.

Here are three examples of *bully* sins.

Example one of a *bully* sin is an *Et tu, Brute?* sin. Shakespeare makes us wince at the diabolical treachery of betrayal by a close friend when he has Caesar say to Brutus 'Even you, Brutus?' as his friend joins his assassins. And

---

13 Matthew 14:30.

14 Genesis 12:10-20 (Abraham); 2 Samuel 12:13 (David); Jonah 2 (Jonah); John 21:15-19 (Peter); Luke 7:47 (The sinful woman).

15 Romans 7:24.

while every sin is a gross betrayal of our best Friend, some cause us a more acute sense of our treachery don't they?

You have a sweet time of prayer and *then* find yourself being unkind to your spouse. The Lord makes your time in the Word burning-bush noteworthy and *then* you refuse to forgive someone who's wronged you. Father keeps a promise in a way that causes you almost to hear Him audibly say, 'I love you!' and *then* you grumble over some little matter that's not going the way you want. Each of these is an '*Et tu, Brute?*' sin, a dagger of disobedience made even more foul by Father's recent kindness to you. *Et tu Brute* sins make you wonder if you can begin again.

Example two of a *bully* sin is an *Achilles' heel* sin. We're all as vulnerable to a wide variety of sins as a soldier is to death on the battlefield during a fierce fight. But each of us also has an area where we're as weak as the Greek warrior's heel was to the arrow that took his life. I confess with sadness that one of my heels is impatience. Sometimes just a small fire makes my kettle boil. Thank God, I've grown some in patience. But I'm still a long way from what I should be. And when I react impatiently to someone or some situation I'm tempted to throw my hands up in hopelessness. Achilles' heel sins make you wonder if you can begin again.

Example three of a *bully* sin is a *Scrooge's ghost* sin. This is some past confessed sin rising up to haunt you the way the miser Scrooge's ghosts haunted him in Dickens' *Christmas Carol*. The strongest example of this I've ever found comes from D. Martyn Lloyd-Jones' ministry. He tells of a seventy-seven-year-old man converted out of a notoriously evil life. The entire church celebrates the day the man joins the church and comes to the Lord's Supper for the first time. Everyone goes home rejoicing. Bright and early the next day the man's at Lloyd-Jones' house abject, weeping, despondent. When Lloyd-Jones asks what's wrong the man relates a time thirty years earlier when he'd been drinking in a pub and had said, 'Jesus Christ was a bastard!' Now this past sin is a Scrooge's ghost haunting him in the present.[16] Scrooge's ghost sins make you wonder if you can begin again.

5.

The good news is the truth that even our bully sins don't leave us in a cul-de-sac of guilt and hopelessness. There is a highway to beginning again for them, too. It's the same 1 John 1:9 highway you take for other sins. Take it with your bully sins because 'the blood of Jesus cleanses us from *ALL* sin.'[17]

Maybe you need to take that highway now. Do so immediately. Confess and be cleansed and restored to fellowship with Father.

If not, and if you're like me, you'll need to travel on it soon. The glory and wonder is the fact that there is an on-ramp onto this highway from every sin you ever commit. Even your bully sin.

Forgiveness through Jesus' blood by confession of sin is the highway to the land of beginning again. Take that highway whenever you need it.

---

16 D. M. Lloyd-Jones, *Spiritual Depression Its Causes and Cures* (Grand Rapids, MI: Wm B. Eerdmans Publishing, Co., 1965), 67-68.

17 1 John 1:7, emphasis added.

18

The Door That's Always Open

Charles Spurgeon was a unique combination of personality and prayer. His multifaceted ministry life fell into orbit around his devotional life. But how did Spurgeon remain devoted to God in the midst of all the distractions that constantly pulled at his attention? How did Spurgeon keep his focus on Jesus Christ amidst the crashing waves of life?…(He) was once told that a man spent three hours on his knees in prayer. Spurgeon responded, 'I could not do it if my eternity depended on it!' Then his friend, William, recalled Spurgeon saying, 'I go to God with a promise, which is in reality a cheque issued by God Himself on the bank of heaven. He cashes it for me, and then I go and use what He has given me, to His glory…I think I can say that seldom many minutes elapse without my heart speaking to God in either prayer or praise.—Keeney Dickenson[1]

Prayer.

How can this gift that ought to make you sing like a nightingale *also* make you groan like a widow at a freshly dug grave? It is *a gift*, second only to the Lord Jesus Himself and

---

1   Keeney Dickenson, *How to Experience God Like Spurgeon*, Spurgeon.org, October 19, 2017.

the indwelling Holy Spirit, isn't it? Yet your prayer life *makes you groan* doesn't it? Who among us doesn't acknowledge that prayer is the subject we struggle most with in the school of discipleship? I've never met a believer who claims to have a PhD in prayer. If I ever do I'm going to pray for him/her!

Is there a way of doing prayer so that it's more of the blessing Father wants it to be in your life? Yes. Jesus shows us there is in His promise, 'Ask, and it will be given to you; seek, and you will find; knock, and it will be opened to you. For everyone who asks receives, and the one who seeks finds, and to the one who knocks it will be opened.'[2]

Remember, the verbs *ask, seek,* and *knock* are each in the *present* tense.[3] Jesus isn't talking about something you do every now and then like your six-month dental checkup. He's talking about something you do every day, all day long like breathing. He's talking about praying our way through our day. He assures us that Father will give us good things as we do. The promise, then, is *Father will give you good things as you pray your way through your day.*

1.

The *content* of this promise is *your Father's assurance that He wants to be graciously involved in your life every day, all day long.* He doesn't want you to live as an abandoned or orphaned child. In fact, He wants you to live a 'dancing,

---

2   Matthew 7:7-8.

3   Stott, *The Message of the Sermon on the Mount*, 184. '(A)ll three verbs are present imperatives and indicate the persistence with which we should make our requests known to God.'

leaping, daring life' as His child.[4] He wants to show you how much He delights in you, how much He enjoys helping you, how much He wishes to get glory from you by being good to you every day, all day long. So He wants you to come to Him continually every day, all day long. That's the point of these verbs being in the present tense. This grammar is Father's invitation to you to come to Him from the time you get up until the time you go to bed so you can *experience* in clear and palpable ways the joy of having Him as your Father.

2.

The *condition* of this promise of experiencing in clear and palpable ways the joy of having Him as your Father every day, all day long, is *praying your way through your day*. The emphasis in verses 7-8 is on *repeated* prayer.[5] Jesus is telling you here to go through your day asking Father to help you as repeatedly as a two-year-old goes through his day saying 'Momma.' You're to pray your way through your day.

3.

How do you pray your way through your day? By praying *brief* prayers. You pray prayers that come out in as few words as a typical teen's answer to his mom's 'How was your day?' Peter models this in his three-worded SOS 'Lord, save me'

---

4   Charles Swindoll, *The Grace Awakening* (Nashville, TN: Thomas Nelson, 1990), 75.

5   Stott writes of verse 7, '… all three verbs are present imperatives and indicate the persistence with which we should make our requests known to God.' *The Message of the Sermon on the Mount*, 184.

cry for help as he sees the wind and begins to sink.[6] The father of the possessed boy disciples you in this brief praying with his five-worded plea, 'I believe; help my unbelief.'[7] And the Lord Jesus Himself epitomizes this with His four-worded cry of dereliction, 'Eli, Eli, Lama Sabachthani?'[8] and His eight-worded, 'Father, into your hands I commit my spirit.'[9] You pray your way through your day by praying again and again, all day long, prayers as brief as those of Peter, the boy's father, and the Lord Jesus.

4.

Why should you pray your way through your day? Because this is a practical and profitable way for you to experience your Father's delight in giving you the good gift of His help.

First, praying your way through your day is *practical*. It can be done in a classroom, boardroom, waiting room, on the golf course, and anywhere and everywhere else. It can be done standing or sitting or walking or driving your car. It can be done silently or orally. It can be done between being asked a question and giving an answer, between being confronted with temptation and giving in, between being given a harsh criticism and responding, between hearing the receptionist say 'The doctor will see you now' and walking into her consulting room.

Second, praying your way through your day is *profitable*. Father delights in answering these prayers. Just as Jesus

---

6   Matthew 14:30.

7   Mark 9:24.

8   Matthew 27:46.

9   Luke 23:46.

answered Peter's brief prayer and the demon-possessed boy's brief prayer, so Father will answer again and again the brief prayers you make as you go through your day. Listen again to Jesus: 'Ask, *and it will be given you*; seek, *and you will find*; knock, *and it will be opened to you.*'

5.

The best way to pray your way through your day with prayers that are brief *and* profitable is by *praying 'Father, you say' prayers every day all day long*. A 'Father, you say' prayer is a prayer that claims a promise and asks the Father to keep it. 'Father, you say if I confess you'll forgive; I confess, please forgive me' (1 John 1:9). 'Father, you say if I ask you for wisdom you'll give it. I ask' (James 1:5). 'Father, you say you'll help me defeat any temptation. Help me say "No!" now' (1 Cor. 10:13). Do this and you'll find yourself praising Father all day long for keeping His promises to you.

6.

Scottish preacher Alexander Whyte delighted in helping the students in his pastor's classes. He knew they would sometimes find life hard. He told them, 'Come to me when your back is to the wall. I will never shut my door against you.'[10] Christian, you have something better. You belong to a Father who never shuts His door. He wants you to come to Him every day all day long for good gifts. You do that by claiming His promise in Matthew 7:7-8 by praying your way through your day.

---

10 G. F. Barbour, *The Life of Alexander Whyte* (London: Hodder and Stoughton Limited, 1923), 336.

Claim this promise and begin praying this way.

Do that and you'll see.

When it comes to you, Father's door is always open.

19

The Promise John Piper Uses to Defeat Fear

How numerous are the admonitions against fear addressed in the Scripture to the Lord's people. And what do all these imply, but their proneness to apprehension, and the groundlessness of their alarms? Hence the injunction is never unaccompanied with an argument to enforce it…But though the Christian may fear, every thing is safe and right with him; and therefore the more he truly examines his condition, the more he must be satisfied with it. His doubts are mistakes, his apprehensions are misapprehensions. He only needs to be informed of things as they really are, and he is free indeed. Hence nothing can be of more importance to the subjects of divine grace than just and clear views of their states and privileges; for though their safety does not depend upon the degree of their knowledge, their consolation is much affected by it. 'They that fear his name will put their trust in him.'—William Jay[1]

Baptist pastor and author John Piper's PhD is from the University of Munich. He was twenty-five years old when he and his wife Noël moved there. They stayed three years while John earned his degree.

---

1 William Jay, *Evening Exercises for Everyday in the Year* (Harrisburg, VA: Sprinkle Publications, 1999), 532.

Piper's evangelist father Bill was unable to see him off due to a speaking engagement. But in a telephone conversation Bill gave his son this *Bon Voyage* promise from Isaiah 41:10 to carry with him: 'Fear not, for I am with you; be not dismayed, for I am your God; I will strengthen you, I will help you, I will uphold you with my righteous right hand.'

Piper testifies that 'for three years in Germany, Isaiah 41:10 was on my lips and in my heart during anxious times more than any other verse.' In fact, he used it so often that it's now so hardwired in his brain that his mind instinctively turns to it when it's in neutral. It's no surprise this heirloom verse was the one he passed along to his son Benjamin when he left for boot camp in Fort Jackson, South Carolina.[2]

Piper testifies that as he used this promise to overcome fear of every kind when it assaulted him he saw 'God again and again come through for me.'[3]

Our brother recommends that we use it too. *In the promise of Isaiah 41:10 Father offers to do us the good of delivering us from fear.*

1.

The *content* of this promise is *deliverance from fear.* One Sunday morning at London's Westminster Chapel during WWII the congregation is joined in public worship by a most unwelcome visitor. The building is shaken by the exploding payload a German bomber drops nearby. It goes off while Dr. Martyn Lloyd-Jones is praying his pastoral

---

2   Piper tells this story in his sermon, 'Fear not, I Am with You, I Am Your God,' http://www.desiringgod.org/messages/fear-not-i-am-with-you-i-am-your-god. June 20, 1993.

3   Ibid.

prayer. Dust and debris fall from the ceiling. People in the chapel's upper tiers are frightened. Their pastor isn't. The doctor pauses from praying, looks up, gently tells everyone not to panic but quietly to come down and be seated on the first floor. He then returns to his prayer. His courage calms everyone. A WWI veteran of trench warfare is present that day. He says he's not seen on the battlefield anything braver than Lloyd-Jones' actions. Lloyd-Jones' biographer says the doctor was simply acting as someone who really believed that because he belonged to God he had no reason to fear.[4]

Father Himself is telling us in Isaiah 41:10 that because we belong to Him we have nothing to fear. We need to hear this don't we? It's often said that the most repeated commandment in the Bible is 'Fear not!' This is due to the fact that fear is both prevalent and perilous.

Fear is *prevalent*. We're spooked as easily as a skittish horse. We're as quickly startled by various things as we are by someone unexpectedly walking up behind us. We become alarmed in the twinkling of an eye when we feel a lump in a thigh, face a decision that won't sit well with an employer asking us to do something unethical, think about certain politicians running the government and a thousand and one other things.

Fear is *perilous*. Fear led Abraham to lie and compromise the honor of God and the safety of his wife.[5] Fear led Elijah to temporarily abandon his post and writhe in self-pity.[6]

---

4   Iain Murray, *D. Martyn Lloyd-Jones: The Fight of Faith 1939-1981* (Edinburgh: The Banner of Truth Trust, 1990), 114-115.

5   Genesis 12:11-20.

6   1 Kings 19.

Fear led the disciples to panic in a storm and question the Savior's concern for them.[7] Fear led Peter to deny the Savior three times.[8] Fear led many Jewish Christians to consider abandoning the faith because of persecution.[9] And that's just skimming the surface of this evil's bad influence. You're seldom in graver danger than when you're afraid.

Franklin D. Roosevelt's wise words to Americans amid wartime apprehensions apply to us as believers: 'We have nothing to fear but fear itself.'[10] Yet that's sometimes hard to believe isn't it? That's why we ought to thank Father for His promise in Isaiah 41:10. Alec Motyer says Father gives us in these words this fear-defeating assurance: 'Yes, I will strengthen you! Indeed, I will help you! Why, I will uphold you!'[11] Father is assuring us that since He is bigger than anything we fear and will help us handle what we fear we have no reason to be afraid of anything at any time. Claim this promise and you will frighten fear and make it cower before you like the demons groveling before the Lord Jesus whenever He confronts them in the Gospels.[12]

2.

The *condition* for claiming this promise is *taking it at face value*. Simply put, take Father at His word. Believe that He

---

7   Mark 4:38.

8   Mark 14:66-72.

9   The Book of Hebrews.

10   William J. Bennett, *America: The Last Best Hope* (Nashville, TN: Thomas Nelson, 2007), 109.

11   J. Alec Motyer, *The Prophecy of Isaiah: An Introduction & Commentary* (Downers Grove, IL: InterVarsity Press, 1993), 312.

12   Mark 1:23-26; Mark 5:7-8.

stands behind His pledge and will honor it every time you claim this promise. Demonstrate you believe it by raising it as a shield by saying it aloud whenever the fiery darts of fear assault you. Do that and you'll find fear turning its tail and running like an escaped convict who hears the howling of hounds on his trail.

3.

The time to *claim* this promise is *anytime you're afraid*. Piper says he regularly claimed it as he rode his bike to class knowing he might be called upon to participate in German. I'm claiming it now as I fight fear over a medical procedure I'm having in two days. Claim it as you face aging and the fiends inhabiting it or begin living alone after being deserted by your spouse or go through bypass surgery or shrink before the increasing antagonism to Christianity that snarls and snaps everywhere you turn.

4.

I was a late bloomer physically. I'm 5'11" now but from the age of thirteen to fifteen I was about 5'3". My smallness made me an easy target for the schoolyard bully in middle school. He started on me at recess the first day. But I had a friend named Dan. As early as the seventh grade, Dan was tall and built like something Michelangelo had chiseled out of marble. He looked like a mini Muhammad Ali. Like Ali, Dan was tough and fearless and could float like a butterfly and sting like a bee. When he found out about my bully he took him aside and warned him, 'If you ever touch Charley Chase again I'm coming after you.' The bullied bully never bullied me again.

Isaiah 41:10 is your Dan promise for the bully of fear. John Piper found it tough enough to scare away the fears of living and studying in a foreign country. Father assures you you'll find it big enough to handle whatever frightens you.

20
The Fork in the Road

How great and honourable is the privilege of a true believer!
That he has neither wisdom nor strength in himself, is no
disadvantage; for he is connected with infinite wisdom and
almighty power…and though he be fallible and short-sighted,
exceedingly liable to mistake and imposition; yet, while
he retains a sense that he is so, and with the simplicity of a
child asks counsel and direction of the Lord, he seldom takes
a wrong step, at least not in matters of consequence; and even
his inadvertencies are overruled for good.—John Newton[1]

Yogisms.

Those seemingly nonsensical statements made by
New York Yankee Hall of Fame Catcher Yogi Berra that,
examined, make sense. Here's one of my favorites: 'When
you come to a fork in the road take it!' And you do, don't
you? Forks in the road confront you with a choice. And you
make choices again and again.

Your choices are important. The late UCLA basketball
coach John Wooden was fond of saying, 'There's a choice

---

1   John Newton, *The Works of John Newton, Volume I* (Edinburgh: The
    Banner of Truth Trust, 2015), 370.

you have to make / in everything you do / so keep in mind that in the end / the choice you make makes you.'[2]

Choosing wisely is essential to living Father's way. So, how do you make wise choices? By using the promise Father gives you in James 1:5-8:

> If any of you lacks wisdom, let him ask God, who gives generously to all without reproach, and it will be given him. But let him ask in faith, with no doubting, for the one who doubts is like a wave of the sea that is driven and tossed by the wind. For that person must not suppose that he will receive anything from the Lord; he is a double-minded man, unstable in all his ways.

In this promise Father offers to do you the good of giving you wisdom.

1.

The *content* of this promise is 'wisdom.' God paints a masterpiece of wisdom on the canvas of a decision made by King Solomon.[3] You're familiar with the story. Two prostitutes bring Solomon a paternity conflict that's as baffling as a cold case homicide detectives have given up trying to solve. Each woman gives birth to a child. During the night one mother accidently kills her child (apparently by rolling on him as she sleeps). She wakes, sees her dead child, lifts him, creeps into the room where the other woman and her child are sleeping, and exchanges children with pickpocket deftness.

---

2   Movemequotes.com. Top 15 John Wooden Quotes.

3   This story is told in 1 Kings 3:18-28. It's important for a reader to know that it comes as an example of the truth that God gave Solomon the wisdom he asked for in 3:1-17.

In the morning the mother of the living child realizes the dead child isn't hers. So, the women appear before Solomon with the living child—a rope in a macabre tug of war—as each insists the child is hers. Compounding the mystery is the fact that there are no eyewitnesses to back up either woman's claim.

A real head-scratching teasing conundrum, huh? Not for Solomon. He calls for a sword and tells a guard to cut the child in two and give a half to each woman. The moment he speaks, the biological mother pleads that the child be spared and given to the other woman while the other woman consents to the verdict coldly. Solomon immediately gives the child to its real mother.

What's happened? Solomon has solved *The Mystery of the Maternal Mixup* with an adroitness that Agatha Christie would envy. When Israel hears of their King's savvy they understand that he's displayed 'the wisdom of God.'[4]

What does this teach you about wisdom? That *wisdom is doing what's best in a particular situation.* Solomon did what was best (finding out the real mother) in a particular situation (a seemingly impossible to resolve 'she said / she said' dispute). So, Father's promise of wisdom in James 1:5 is His promise that He'll help you do what's best in your particular forks in the road. That is, He's promising to help you make decisions and choices and handle circumstances and situations (both in times of trial and elsewhere) in ways that enable you to glorify and enjoy Him.

---

4   1 Kings 3:28.

2.

There are two *conditions* you must meet if you want Father to give you wisdom.

Condition one is '*asking God*' to give it to you. 'If any of you lack wisdom, let him ask God.' Like the Gospel itself, this seems too simple to be true. But it isn't. The fruit of wisdom is found in the orchard of prayer. Solomon got wisdom by asking. You'll get it by asking too.

Condition two is asking God *with optimism*. You're to 'ask in faith.' Don't ask God for wisdom with the 'it's a long shot' mentality the least popular boy in high school has as he asks the homecoming queen for a date. Ask with the 'it's a sure thing' mentality the star QB has as he asks her. Father wants you to ask knowing that wisdom 'will be given' you when you ask. In fact, He wants you to be sure you can no more ask Him for wisdom and go away without it than you can truly trust Jesus for salvation and not be forgiven.

James gives you three reasons for asking this optimistically. Each echoes Jesus' encouraging promise in Matthew 7:11.

The first reason you should optimistically ask Father for wisdom is *His description of Himself as the 'God who gives.'* Like a poor painting covering a masterpiece, these words hide a treasure underneath. The better translation is 'the giving God.' Giving to you is Father's delight. He's so disposed to give to you that He makes a doting grandmother seem as reluctant to help her grandson as a proud man is to admit he's wrong. That should make you optimistic every time you ask Him for wisdom.

The second reason you should optimistically ask Father for wisdom is *His 'generosity.'* Generosity is Father's middle name. He'll give you wisdom as *freely* as you give your children what they want at Christmas and as *fully* as you fill your car's gas tank before leaving on a trip. He'll give you all the wisdom you need when you ask. That should make you optimistic every time you ask Him for wisdom.

The third reason you should optimistically ask Father for wisdom is *His magnanimity.* He gives 'without reproach.' He won't scold you for not asking Him as quickly as you should have. He won't treat your request the way you'd treat the request of a neighbor who has borrowed ten tools and kept them now asking you to loan him your shovel. Father gives you His word that He won't let your past conduct dam the flow of His generosity in your present need. He'll *always* treat you the way the prodigal's father treated his returning son. That should make you optimistic every time you ask Him for wisdom.

3.

When should you *claim* this promise? All the time. This is one of those promises we ought to be constantly claiming. Anytime you're not sure how to act in a way that glorifies Father and is good for you and others, ask Him for wisdom. Ask for wisdom as a Christian. Ask for wisdom as a parent. Ask for wisdom as a single person. Ask for wisdom as a married person. Ask for wisdom as an employer. Ask for wisdom as an employee. Ask for wisdom when making decisions. And ask for wisdom when you are in a trial. Start your day asking for wisdom and go through your day asking for wisdom.

Ask for wisdom and Father will do you the good of helping you know which fork in the road you should take when you come to it.

21

A Dealer in Hope

Years ago Saturday newspapers routinely carried the sermon topics for the next day in the leading pulpits in town. In Norfolk, Virginia, Reverend R. I. Williams of Fairmont Park Methodist Church picked up the phone and called the local paper to give them his sermon topic. 'The Lord is my Shepherd,' he said. The person on the other end said, 'Is that all?' Reverend Williams replied, 'That's enough.' The next day the church page carried his sermon topic as 'The Lord is my Shepherd—That's Enough!'—Robert J. Morgan[1]

A well-known legend about the devil speaks a profound truth. I'll retell it in modern language.

His infernal majesty puts the tools of his trade up for sale. Table after table displays the wicked wonders of his workshop. Lust and jealousy and pride and hatred and bitterness are showcased next to the other hellish devices he's used for centuries with serpentine subtlety. But one tool— ordinary looking as a screwdriver and worn as a threadbare rug—is on a table by itself. Surprisingly, it's priced ten times higher than any of the others. The tool? *Discouragement.*

---

1   Robert J. Morgan, *The Lord Is My Shepherd* (New York, NY: Howard Books, 2013), xiv-xv.

Asked, 'Why the exorbitant price for such a dilapidated tool?' Satan answers, 'Because discouragement's my go-to tool. When I can't get inside a person's heart with any of the others, it gets me in as easily as I got access to Eve in the Garden. And once I'm in through discouragement I can control the person as easily as the flu controls someone it's invaded. It's badly worn for a simple reason. I've used it successfully again and again.'

Rings true, doesn't it? Satan conquers thousands with greed and lust and anger. But he subdues tens of thousands with discouragement. It's as common among believers as weeds in a vacant lot. Who among us has never been a P.O.W. in the Andersonville squalor of the blues? Maybe that's why Napoleon says, 'A leader is a dealer in hope.'[2] Father is our leader. And in the cluster of promises He gives us in Psalm 23 He deals us all the hope we need in our most acute times of discouragement.[3]

In the promise to be your Shepherd, Father offers you the good of discouragement-conquering hope.

1.

We start with the *condition* for claiming this promise. The condition for claiming it is the *recognition of what discouragement is.* You'll no more defeat discouragement without understanding what it is than a mechanic can fix

---

2   H. A. Dorfman, *Coaching the Mental Game* (New York, NY: Taylor Trade Publishing, 2003), 38.

3   I take 'The Lord is my shepherd' to be the central promise of Psalm 23. The rest of the Psalm explains what's involved in this promise, i.e. that Father will care for us with the all-encompassing care a shepherd bestows on his sheep.

your car until he understands exactly what's wrong with it or a doctor can help you get well without an accurate diagnosis of what's wrong with you. So, what's going on when you're discouraged?

Bring your seat back into upright position, put up your tray table, and buckle your seat belt because the next few paragraphs will be bumpy.

Ready?

Here goes: *when you're discouraged you're doing nothing less than telling Father that you're wiser than He is.* In fact, you're insisting that this is the case as forcefully as the Pharisees insisted that they knew better than Jesus what true religion is all about.

Investigate a season of discouragement closely and you'll find that discouragement is always a suit filed against Father for one of two reasons. He's either *not given to you* or He's *taken from you* something you're convinced *is best for you.* Here are examples of each form of discouragement.

A.

A single Christian mopes miserably because he/she longs to be married but is still single and not getting any younger…a couple sings the blues because they yearn for children but remain childless while their biological clock ticks away and their married friends all seem to be advertisements for the power of fertility drugs… a high school basketball player licks his/her wounds because a lifelong dream of playing at the next level isn't going to happen…In each case these believers are discouraged because Father isn't *giving to them* something they think is *best* for them. Surely your discouragement sees itself in their mirror. I assure you mine does.

B.

A believer is downcast because, due to loss of enrollment, she's let go from a teaching position she loves…an older preacher is crippled with despondency because he feels he's more useful than he's ever been but retirement's taken away preaching opportunities that other retired ministers seem to have in bunches…a Christian advertising company's number one client for the past fifteen years decides to give his business to a competitor…In each case these believers are discouraged because *something's being taken from them* that they think is *best* for them. Surely your discouragement sees itself in their mirror. I assure you mine does.

You must grasp that when you're discouraged you're 'leaning on your own understanding.'[4] You're thinking that something that's best for you is either being withheld from you or being taken from you. This notion is the taproot for *every* discouragement. And it's nothing less than the ugly insistence that you know better than Father what's best for you.

Serious stuff, huh? But until we see that this is what our discouragement's all about we'll be like an alcoholic who hasn't come to the point of desperation that makes him do what needs to be done to stop drinking.

---

4   See Proverbs 3:5.

2.

The *content* of the anti-discouragement promise Father gives you is the *assurance that the One who is fully responsible for you WANTS what's best for you, KNOWS what's best for you, and is ALWAYS DOING what's best for you.* This is the message of Psalm 23. And Psalm 23 is the penicillin for the infection of discouragement.

> The Lord is my shepherd; I shall not want.
>   He makes me lie down in green pastures.
> He leads me beside still waters.
>   He restores my soul.
> He leads me in paths of righteousness
>   for his name's sake.
>
> Even though I walk through the valley of the shadow of death,
>   I will fear no evil,
> for you are with me;
>   your rod and your staff,
>   they comfort me.
>
> You prepare a table before me
>   in the presence of my enemies;
> you anoint my head with oil;
>   my cup overflows.
> Surely goodness and mercy shall follow me
>   all the days of my life,
> and I shall dwell in the house of the Lord
>   forever.

It's easy to fall into the not-seeing-the-forest-because-of-the-trees error with this Psalm. You can get so mesmerized by the minutia of the metaphor that you fail to hear its basic message. That message can be summarized in two encouraging truths.

Encouraging truth one that summarizes the message of Psalm 23: *Father assumes full responsibility for our welfare.* That's what it means for Him to be our 'Shepherd.' Notice the emphasis, throughout the Psalm, on Father's hands-on, continuous care, pervasive provision/protection, and solicitous supervision of our lives. In calling Himself our Shepherd Father is telling each of us, 'I assume full responsibility for protecting you, providing for you, and preserving you.' Cole Porter sang about needing 'Someone to watch over me.' You've got the greatest Someone there is watching over you!

Encouraging truth two that summarizes the message of Psalm 23: *Father is always doing what's best for us.* Reread the Psalm and you'll see that its point is that a shepherd is committed to the welfare of his sheep. He's always doing what's in the best interest of every sheep in his flock. In calling Himself our Shepherd Father is telling each of us, 'I *want* what's best for you even more than you do. I *know* what's best for you even more than you do. And I'm *always and only doing* what's best for you even when I don't give you something you want or allow you to lose something you prize.' Verse six sums up this truth wonderfully: the Lord's '*goodness and mercy*' accompany every moment of your earthly life. Even what's discouraging you at this moment is in this hope-giving category.

3

The *condition* for experiencing the good of this promise is *resting in the sheer word of your Father.* The writer of Proverbs helps you here. Proverbs 3:5-6 tells you, 'Trust in the Lord with all your heart, and do not lean on your own understanding. In all your ways acknowledge him, and he will make straight your paths.'

Psalm 23 urges us to trust that Father is dealing with us in goodness and mercy *in the very thing that's disappointing us.* In spite of what we think, in spite of how things seem to us, in spite of how we feel—especially when everything seems to deny that Father is being good to us—we're to rest in Father's sheer word of promise that He's up to our good in our disappointments.

Peter models this type of acting on the basis of the sheer word of the Lord. He's fished all night and caught nothing. Jesus tells him to throw out his nets again. Frustrated over a fishless night, muscles aching, body craving sleep, Peter says, 'Master, we toiled all night and took nothing!' Still, he submits to the sheer word of the Lord: 'But at your word I will let down the nets.' He does and you know the rest of the story. They catch so many fish their nets begin breaking.[5]

Walk in your cousin Peter's footsteps when you're discouraged, Christian. Turn to your Father and say, 'Father, I don't see how this situation's best for me. But you promise me in Psalm 23 that you're always doing what's best for me. In spite of what I think and feel, I rest in your sheer word. I take what you say at face value. I rest in your assurance that

---

5   Luke 5:4-7.

it's best for me not to have what you haven't given or what you've taken away.'

The truth that Father is our Shepherd gives us reason for encouragement no matter what's going on in our lives.

4.

You *claim* this promise to defeat discouragement by realizing how ludicrous it is to live as if you know what's best for you better than your Father does. Allan Emery shows you a more excellent way. He's spending a night with a Texas shepherd and his flock of 2,000. Spring has recently melted winter's snow. The grass is greening. Night's fallen and the shepherd's built a bonfire. The sheep have settled in for the night but are soon wakened by the wail of coyotes. The sheep are scared. The shepherd tosses more logs on the fire and it glows brighter. That's when Allan sees what Psalm 23 is all about. He looks out in the bonfire's glow and sees thousands of tiny lights. The fire's being reflected in the sheep's eyes. And all the eyes are *looking in one direction—at the shepherd.*[6]

That's what Father wants you to do when you're discouraged. He deals you hope in Psalm 23. You can say, 'The Lord is my Shepherd.' And that means your Father—the wisest and most powerful Person in existence—is up to your good in what's discouraging you.

Our Father is our Shepherd. That truth is a dealer of hope in our most disappointing disappointments.

---

6   Morgan, 31-32.

22

Is Romans 8:28 Still in the Bible?

To know that nothing hurts the godly, is a matter of comfort; but to be assured that ALL things which fall out shall co-operate for their good, that their crosses shall be turned into blessings, that showers of affliction water the withering root of their grace and make it flourish more; this may fill their hearts with joy till they run over.—Thomas Watson[1]

A Christian 'knows himself to be God's child, adopted, beloved, secure, with his inheritance awaiting him and eternal joy guaranteed. He knows that nothing can separate him from the love of God in Christ, nor dash him from his Saviour's hand, and that nothing can happen to him which is not for his long-term good, making him more like Jesus and bringing him ultimately closer to God. So when fears flood his soul, as they do the soul of every normal person from time to time, he drives them back by reminding himself of these things ...'—J. I. Packer[2]

---

1   Thomas Watson, *All Things For Good* (Edinburgh: The Banner of Truth Trust, 1986 reprint), 8.

2   J. I. Packer, *God's Words* (Downers Grove, IL: InterVarsity Press, 1981), 107.

It's time to face the elephant in the room. How's Father up to our good in the *really, really, really bad things* that happen to us?

That's a tough question. But one that Father answers. What's His answer?

1.

First of all, *Father doesn't deny that we may well go through bad things*. He doesn't engage in spin or walk back this hard truth. Just the opposite. He says about us what Shelby Foote says about President of the Confederacy Jefferson Davis: 'He had known tears in his time.'[3] Father tells you candidly that you're going to know tears too. And sometimes the tears may flow because really, really, really bad things have happened to you. Some may already have. And more may be on the way, heading toward you like a category five hurricane brewing in the Gulf, small as a thumbnail on the radar now but soon to blow over you with Federal Disaster Area savagery. Jesus tells you, 'In the world you will have tribulation' and Peter says that tribulation may sometimes be a 'fiery trial.'[4] Really, really, really bad things sometimes happen to Father's children.

What kind of bad things? All the East of Eden ills that afflict unbelievers with whom we share life in this sin-cursed world filled with the 'tears' of 'enmity…pain…thorns…

---

3   Shelby Foote, *First Blood—The Thing Gets Under Way* (New York: Random House, 1958), 5.

4   John 16:33; 1 Peter 4:12.

thistles.'[5] Here are seven examples of the kind of bad believers' experience.

Like unbelievers, some believers experience the death of children. David, the man after God's own heart, lost Absalom.[6] Job, the man God describes as the most God-fearing person on the earth during his lifetime, lost ten children.[7] While I don't share David's and Job's sanctity I do share their sorrow. I have lost two grandsons. You may experience this too.

Like unbelievers, some believers die suddenly and, humanly speaking, tragically in their youth. The Methuselah-long life we all desire is snatched from them as easily as a pickpocket lifts a wallet. Believing Abel is the victim of the first homicide;[8] godly Jonathan is sent home from battle in a flag draped coffin;[9] and countless young believers die on foreign battle fields or at the hands of drunk drivers or through some freak accident. You may experience this too.

Like unbelievers, some believers experience personal economic Black Fridays. Like Job, in a moment, in the twinkling of an eye, everything they've worked for is lost.[10] A market plummets and this devours their retirement like a snake swallowing a frog. The house they thought was a bull market investment turns into a bear that's eventually sold at

---

5   Tears, Revelation 21:4; Enmity, etc., Genesis 3:15-18.

6   2 Samuel 18:31-33.

7   Job 1:18-19.

8   Genesis 4:8.

9   1 Samuel 31:2.

10 Job 1.

a whopping loss. Their company's belt-tightening squeezes them out of their job. You may experience this too.

Like unbelievers, some believers live their whole lives as single people. They don't want this any more than a man crawling through the Sahara wants to die of thirst. They'd give anything to walk down an aisle in a gloriously decorated church and say, 'I do' to the person of their dreams. But it never happens. They live their entire adult lives and go to their graves without anything even remotely close to a serious romantic relationship, coming home night after lonely night to an empty home or apartment. Or, maybe even worse, they find themselves in one or more serious relationships they think are altar bound but find each ending up with them nursing a broken heart—again. You may experience this too.

Like unbelievers, some believers experience a life-hampering, happiness-debilitating issue that makes everyday living a struggle. Some have a child with a congenital defect or crippling disease that makes daily living always a chore and sometimes a nightmare for both parent and child. Some have a Joni Eareckson-type accident that leaves them paralyzed. Some have a Paul-like thorn in the flesh that nags them all their days. You may experience this too.

Like unbelievers, some believers commit shameful sins. The Bible is full of tarnished halo believers from drunken Noah to adulterous David to rebellious Jonah to man-fearing Peter.[11] These sins wound Father's honor and hurt Father's people. You may experience this too.

---

11 Genesis 9:18-28 (Noah); 2 Samuel 11:4-5 (David); Jonah 1:3 (Jonah); Matthew 26:69-75 (Peter).

Like unbelievers, some believers are wronged with wrong so foul, so ugly, so degrading that it leaves a wound that only amazing grace can heal. They're victimized and violated and abused and assaulted as Joseph was by his brothers and Potiphar's wife, Samson was at the hands of the Philistines who put out his eyes and made him grind at their mill, and Stephen was when he was callously stoned by a Christianity-hating mob.[12] Many Christians know the horrors of verbal, sexual, and racial abuse. You may experience this too.

Here is reality for you as a believer: Nowhere in the Bible does Father tell you that bad things won't happen to you because you're His child. Just the opposite. He candidly assures us that He allows these kinds of things to invade the lives of the people He loves most.

There's something grand about His integrity about this, isn't there? Can't you trust a Father who has no fine print in His contract, who tells you openly and candidly that belonging to Him doesn't give you an unlisted number when it comes to the obscene caller of really, really, really bad things happening to you? A Father this honest is worthy of your trust through thick and thin.

2.

Thankfully, this isn't all that Father says to us about the really, really, really bad things that may befall us. *He also makes us a panacea promise.* A panacea is a remedy for anything and everything. God's panacea promise is the remedy for everything that happens to you. He makes it in Romans

---

12   Genesis 37 and 39 (Joseph); Judges 16:21 (Samson); Acts 7:54-60 (Stephen).

8:28: 'And we know that in all things God works for the good of those who love him, who have been called according to his purpose.'

In this promise Father makes available to us the good gift of assurance that He will do something so extraordinary with EVERY bad thing that we face that we will one day praise Him for that bad thing.

A.

The *content* of this promise is stunning: *Father wants you to be optimistic that He is micromanaging your life so that everything you experience furthers your best interest by making you more and more like Jesus.* This can be broken into five crisp assurances from Father.

Father is *micromanaging* your life. You aren't a leaf blown by the wind of luck. You aren't the master of your fate or the captain of your soul. You aren't a slave controlled by the whims of the powerful. And you aren't a puppet on strings pulled by Satan. You're the pride and joy of God's providence. That's what the words 'work together' tell you. Father has the final say-so about what happens to you.

Father is micromanaging your life with your *best interests* in mind. 'Good' means your supreme and ultimate good, the best thing that can happen to you. It includes what's best for you spiritually, physically, emotionally, relationally, geographically, and eternally. Your best good is summed up in the glorious words, God 'will wipe away every tear from their eyes, and death shall be no more, neither shall there be mourning nor crying nor pain anymore, for the former things have passed away.'[13]

Father is micromanaging your life *so that you become more and more like Jesus.* The best thing that can happen to you isn't an earthly life characterized by enough expendable income to buy what you want, from iPads to big screen TVs to SUVs with state of the art gadgetry, while also living on this earth a pain-free, healthy life that ends with a comfortable retirement in an upscale Palm Beach community. The best thing that can happen to you is enjoying the pleasures and treasures that come from glorifying and enjoying Father on the New Earth. And Father says this can happen to you only as you are perfectly and permanently 'conformed to the image of his Son.'[14] So, He's working to make you more like Jesus in character (the kind of person you are) and conduct (the way you speak and act) so that your tears can ultimately be wiped away.[15]

Father is micromanaging your life so that *everything you experience furthers* your best interest *by contributing to your*

---

13 Revelation 21:4.

14 Romans 8:29.

15 The ONLY way to be happy is to be like Jesus. When you are perfectly and permanently like Him you will be perfectly and permanently happy because everything that tarnishes, mars, stains, disturbs, diminishes, corrodes, hinders happiness as a cold hinders enjoying a good meal will be gone. And when you are perfectly and permanently like Jesus everything that provides, promotes, protects, and preserves happiness will be yours forever. Father's way of making you happy is by making you like Jesus because *there is no other way.* The result of Romans 8:29 ('conformed to the image of his Son') is Revelation 21:4 ('He shall wipe away all tears from their eyes').

becoming more like Jesus. There's a scene in a detective movie when the detective responds to something said to him with 'Umm.' The other person asks, 'What's that mean?' The detective says, 'It means Umm.' What's 'all things' in Romans 8:28 mean? It means *ALL THINGS!*[16] Father is assuring you in this promise that He'll 'work' literally, absolutely, categorically, and inclusively everything you experience—including *all the bad things we considered earlier* from your monumental failures to the trials that make you feel like a victim in a horror movie—to the good of your becoming more like His beloved Son. He makes *all things* work together for your good.

Father *wants you to be optimistic* that this is *true for you because you're a Christian.* You *are* described in the words 'them that love God' aren't you? No, you don't love Him as passionately, perfectly, and persistently as you wish. But you *can* (and do!) say to Him what Peter said to Jesus, 'Lord, you know all things; you know that I love you,' can't you?

You can say this because you've been 'called.' With Paul you say, 'Not I but Christ' and rest your entire relationship with God on Jesus' life and Jesus' death. Trusting Jesus this way means that you're included in God's glory through grace 'purpose.' And the way He fulfils His purpose of getting glory from you by being good to you is by making everything you experience further your transformation into a Christlike man or woman. The ability to say 'I am a

---

16 John Calvin writes, 'First, then, let my readers grasp that providence means not that by which God idly observes from heaven what takes place on earth, but that by which as keeper of the keys, *he governs all events.' Institutes 1* (Philadelphia: The Westminster Press, 1960), 202.

Christian' gives you the right and privilege of saying 'Father is working everything for my good.'

Laurie Beth Jones learned from James Autrey the leadership principle she calls 'the presumption of good will.' Autrey had a staff member with the uncanny ability to bring calm and cooperation to people in a company at odds with each other. He did this by opening meetings with the tempest silencing words, 'Now, let's presume everyone here has goodwill toward each other, and proceed from there.'[17]

Father tells you that you don't need to presume He has good will towards you. As a believer in Jesus you can be sure of His goodwill. That goodwill is His determination to get glory from you by giving grace to you. He gives grace to you by being good to you every day all day long. And one of the ways He's good to you every day, all day long is by working your really, really, really bad experiences to the good of making you more like Jesus.

B.

The *condition* for this promise is *optimism* that Father will keep this promise. This promise is the best motivational speech you will ever hear. It's calculated to make you 'more than conqueror'[18] over the worst of your pains, problems, and perplexities. It can calm and comfort you and give you peace and patience 'when all things seem against you to drive you to despair.' But the *enjoyment* of these good gifts depends on your optimism that Father has the will and skill to keep this promise. Without this optimism the promise

---

17 Laurie Beth Jones, *Jesus CEO* (New York, New York: Hyperion, 1992), 268.

18 Romans 8:37.

will no more comfort you than a picture of a Thanksgiving Day feast will satisfy your hunger.

But, truth be told, this is probably the hardest of Father's promises to believe. So, you've got to 'know' that all things work together for your good. Not 'hope' in the lame sense of that word in our ordinary usage as we say on a cloudy day 'I hope the picnic today isn't rained out.' No, you've got to be as sure that Father is keeping this promise as you are that Jesus is God's Son.

What can give you such ironclad assurance when your mind is perplexed and your heart is reeling because you're being pummeled by some horrendous heartache? THE GREAT IMPOSSIBILITY: *It's impossible for your Father to lie!*[19] This is what makes R. C. Sproul's drill-sergeant blunt statement 'For the Christian, every tragedy is ultimately a blessing, or God is a liar'[20] so powerful and comforting. Father can't lie. Father won't lie. He never has. He never will. This gives you reason to be optimistic that He *WILL* work your most painful and perplexing experiences to the good of making you like Jesus.

C.

Obviously, the time to *claim* this promise is when something is going on in your life that tortures and torments you. Again, sooner or later those times will probably come your way in some shape or form. The Bible goes so far as to use a slap-in-the-face-strong word to describe the severity of trial you may

---

19   Numbers 23:19; Hebrews 6:19.

20   R. C. Sproul, *The Invisible Hand: Do All Things Really Work for Good?* (Phillipsburg, NJ: P&R Publishing Company, 1996), 174.

have to endure. It speaks of Father sometimes 'scourging'[21] His children. You may well find yourself in a domestic or romantic or economic heartache that makes you feel like you're being lashed with a leather-thronged whip with each thong laced with pieces of metal. It's then that the question of questions must be asked.

What's that question? Pastor Robert J. Morgan passes it along to you. He's attending a retirement dinner for a CEO friend named Sam. Champagne kudos flow. Morgan finds one a special vintage. The incoming CEO tells of his predecessor's consistent reaction when he had to give him bad financial news. 'Sam would study the gloomy report then look up and say, "Let me ask you, my friend, is Romans 8:28 still in the Bible?" The carrier of bad news would say, "Yes." And Sam would say, "Then this will turn around; it will all work out for good. Don't be discouraged."'[22]

Christian, this is the question of questions for you when 'all things seem against you to drive you to despair.' Is Romans 8:28 still in your Bible?

Is it? Then claim it with optimism that whatever is hurting you now will one day make you say 'Hallellujah!' as you see how Father used it to give you the best good He could give you by causing it to make you more like Jesus.

---

21 The KJV rightly translates Hebrews 12:6 with 'For whom the Lord loveth he chasteneth, and scourgeth every son whom he receiveth.' The original word translated 'scourgeth' is the word for a literal scourging.

22 Robert J. Morgan, *The Promise* (Nashville, TN: B&H Publishing Group, 2010), 39.

3.

When you begin immediately using this and the other seven promises we've considered to enjoy the good Father makes available to you *now* you've taken **Step Three** to becoming acquainted with Father the way He desires. Go ahead and take this step now. Surely at this very moment you need one of the eight promises in chapters thirteen through twenty. Surely you need your optimism strengthened or ability to say 'No' to temptation or forgiveness for a fresh sin or a renewal of your prayer life or help in defeating fear or wisdom in making a decision or grace to overcome discouragement or strength to carry a deep heartache. Find the promise offering you the good you need *now*, meet its condition, and claim it from your Father.

Do that and you'll see. Father means it when He tells you 'Taste and see that the Lord is good.'[23]

Then begin using promises to enjoy Fatherly good every day all day long. Do this and you'll come to know Him as He wants you to know Him.

You'll begin knowing Him as your good, good Father!

One final question needs answering.

Why does Father use the M.O. of giving good gifts through promises? We look at this in the last chapter.

---

23   Psalm 34:8.

Conclusion: Good, Good Father

I walked in the sunshine with a scholar who had effectively forfeited his prospects of academic advancement by clashing with church dignitaries over the gospel of grace. 'But it doesn't matter,' he said at length, 'for I've known God and they haven't.' The remark was a mere parenthesis, a passing comment on something I had said, but it has stuck with me and set me thinking. Not many of us, I think, would ever naturally say that we have known God. The words imply a definiteness and matter-of-factness of experience to which most of us, if we are honest, have to admit that we are still strangers... What were we made for? To know God. What aim should we set ourselves in life? To know God. What is 'the eternal life' that Jesus gives? Knowledge of God (John 17:3). What is the best thing in life, bringing more joy, delight and contentment than anything else? Knowledge of God (Jeremiah 9:23-24). What, of all the states God ever sees man in, gives God most pleasure? Knowledge of himself (Hosea 6:6 KJV).—J. I. Packer.[1]

---

1   J. I. Packer, *Knowing God* (Downers Grove, IL: InterVarsity Press, 1973), 24.

I first heard Chris Tomlin's song *Good, Good Father* when Father took my grandson Andrew James Chase in His gentle arms and brought him to be with Jesus after four and a half days of difficult earthly life. The song was a musical Good Samaritan to our family as we lay bleeding on our Jericho Road of grief.

The song's refrain is the best Father's Day card I've ever read. Here it is:

> You're a good good father
> It's who you are, it's who you are, it's who you are
> And I'm loved by you
> It's who I am, it's who I am, it's who I am.[2]

In my opinion, what gives the song its spiritual impact is the fact that it echoes the opening of Jesus' prayer in John chapter 17: 'When Jesus had spoken these words, he lifted up his eyes to heaven, and said, "Father, the hour has come; glorify your Son that the Son may glorify you, since you have given him authority over all flesh, to give eternal life to all you have given him. *And this is eternal life, that they may know you, the only true God, and Jesus Christ whom you have sent.*"'[3] According to Jesus, eternal life is knowing that through Him God is our good, good Father.

It's in knowing Him this way that we find the answer to the question of why Father uses the M.O. of promises to do us good. Here's that answer: *Father does us good through His promises because He wants us to live in constant enjoyment of the fact that He is our good, good Father.*

---

2   Chris Tomlin, *The Ultimate Playlist*, 2016.

3   John 17:1-3. Emphasis added.

1.

Father wants you to enjoy having Him as your Father. When Jesus says that eternal life is '*knowing the only true God*', He's got something specific in mind.

First, by *knowing* God Jesus is talking about what past generations of Christian writers called '*experimental*' knowledge. Not experimental in the sense of a scientific laboratory testing a hypothesis but experimental in the sense of 'something you know because you've *experienced* it for yourself.' It's the heart of what 'taste' means in the words we looked at earlier: 'Taste and see that the Lord is good.'[4] You taste something when you personally experience it. Jesus wants us to *experience* God in our everyday living.

Second, by knowing *the only true God and Jesus Christ whom (He) has sent* Jesus is talking about experiencing God *as Father*. Experiencing God as Father is the heart of Christlikeness. Read the Gospels, particularly the Gospel of John, and you'll see that Jesus lived in the moment-by-moment awareness that God was His Father. Experiencing God as Father is the reason Father sent Jesus to die for us and the Holy Spirit to live in us.[5] In fact, knowing God as your Father is the essence of what it means to be a Christian. J. I. Packer accurately writes:

> You sum up the whole of the New Testament in a single phrase, if you speak of it as a revelation of the Fatherhood of the holy Creator. In the same way, **you sum up the whole of the New Testament religion if you describe it as the knowledge of God as one's holy Father.** If you want to

---

4   Psalm 34:8.

5   Galatians 4:4-7.

judge how well a person understands Christianity, find out how much he makes of being God's child, and having God as his Father. If this is not the thought that prompts and controls his worship and prayers and his whole outlook on life, it means that he does not understand Christianity very well at all. For everything Christ taught, everything that makes the New Testament new, and better than the Old, everything that is distinctively Christian as opposed to merely Jewish, is summed up in the knowledge of the Fatherhood of God. 'Father' is the Christian name for God.[6]

Packer's paragraph may be the best commentary you'll ever read on Jesus' words 'and this is life eternal that they know you the only true God.' God is truly known only through Jesus and only when He is known as Father.

This is Father's desire for you. He wants you to say of having Him as your Father what David said of Goliath's sword: 'There is none like that.'[7] He wants you to feel that the most loving thing He does for you in Jesus is to become your Father.[8] He wants this truth that He is your Father to multitask in your life by thrilling, comforting, calming, sustaining, and motivating you. He wants this truth that He is your Father to be to you what gold is to a miser, power is to a tyrant, crack is to an addict, a refreshing shower is to a man after a day of yard work in the hot sun, and what Isaac was to Abraham. He wants you to trust Him as your Father,

---

6   Packer, *Knowing God*, 201. Emphasis added.

7   1 Samuel 21:9.

8   1 John 3:1.

love Him as your Father, lean on Him as your Father, glorify Him as your Father, and enjoy Him as your Father.

2.

Father wants you to enjoy having Him as your Father in a conscious way. Again, this is what Jesus is talking about when He talks about *knowing* Father. Enjoying Father as your Father isn't like a drip that medicates and nourishes a patient even while he's in a coma and utterly unaware of what's going on. Enjoying having God as your Father is like being in love. When you're in love you *know* you're in love. You're *conscious* of the fact. You're keenly and profoundly aware of your feelings for the person you love. Even in those times when your love isn't playing with the noisiness of a rock band it's there in the background like Musak in a department store and you can hear it when you focus on it.

It's the same with enjoying Father. It's something that He wants you to be consciously aware of. Sometimes overwhelming you by flooding your heart with gratitude; other times delighting you with the warmth an older couple feel toward each other as they hold hands while walking; other times dimly making its presence known like an old grandfather clock's ticking and chiming; but always to one degree or another, something you're conscious of.

3.

The primary way Father helps us consciously enjoy having Him as Father is through using His promises to experience His Fatherly goodness. Everything about using His promises involves *conscious* action on our part. You must *consciously* use your mind to answer the question, 'What promise speaks to this situation?' You must *consciously* use your mouth to bring the promise to the throne of grace in prayer. You must *consciously* look for the answer with expectancy. And when the good gift comes—as sooner or later it will —you must *consciously* engage in praise.

4.

As you consciously use His promises you begin experiencing the wonder of having Him as Father. It works like this. Consciously using His promises you begin enjoying His good gifts. Consciously enjoying His good gifts you begin feeling how incomparable is your privilege of having Him as your Father. Consciously begin feeling how incomparable is your privilege of having Him as your Father and you will find yourself saying with Job, 'I had heard of you by the hearing of the ear, but now my eye sees you.'[9] Consciously begin saying that of Him and you will have become acquainted with the Father who delights in getting glory from you by being good to you through His promises. You will *feel* that He is your good, good Father and that there is nothing like being loved by Him.

When you become acquainted with God as your good, good Father, you will know Him the way He wants you to know Him. And knowing Him this way will help you to live the abundant life He's secured for you through Jesus.

---

9   Job 42:5.

Christian Focus Publications

Our mission statement —

STAYING FAITHFUL

In dependence upon God we seek to impact the world
through literature faithful to His infallible Word, the
Bible. Our aim is to ensure that the Lord Jesus Christ is
presented as the only hope to obtain forgiveness of sin,
live a useful life and look forward to heaven with Him.

Our books are published in four imprints:

CHRISTIAN
FOCUS

Popular works including biographies, commentaries, basic
doctrine and Christian living.

CHRISTIAN
HERITAGE

Books representing some of the
best material from the rich her-
itage of the church.

MENTOR

Books written at a level suitable
for Bible College and seminary
students, pastors, and other
serious readers. The imprint includes commentaries, doctrinal
studies, examination of current
issues and church history.

CF4•K

Children's books for quality Bible
teaching and for all age groups: Sunday school curriculum, puzzle and
activity books; personal and family
devotional titles, biographies and
inspirational stories — because you
are never too young to know Jesus!

Christian Focus Publications Ltd,
Geanies House, Fearn, Ross-shire,
IV20 1TW, Scotland, United Kingdom.
www.christianfocus.com